THE MAGNOLIA CLUB

THE MAGNOLIA CLUB

"Fine Times with Nature's Finest"

An Anthology of Tales from the Campfires

Compiled and Edited
by
Robert Hitt Neill
and
Elizabeth Rooks

for
The Mississippi Wildlife Federation
P.O. Box 1814
Jackson, MS 39215-1814

Mississippi River Publishing Company
P.O. Drawer 391
Leland, MS 38756

Copyright 1990 by

The Mississippi Wildlife Federation

Published by

Mississippi River Publishing Company
P.O. Drawer 391
Leland, MS 38756

Jacket design by Sam Beibers

Produced by Betsy Harper

Library of Congress
C.I.P. Data Pending

ISBN # 0-9617591-7-8
Printed in Dallas, Texas
by
Taylor Publishing Co.

10 9 8 7 6 5 4 3 2 1

CONTENTS

v

FOREWORD

The Magnolia State has been blessed with a rich tradition of literary talent, and nowhere is this talent more evident than in the field of outdoor writing. It has indeed been a pleasure to work with this heritage, reviewing the submissions from the old masters like Gene Nunnery and Mabry Anderson, to the heretofore "undiscovered" scribes like Jim Ritchie and Paul Meek. Elizabeth Rooks and I are privileged to have been able to put this volume together in a first-of-its-kind collection.

While many of these stories are of hunting experiences, we all know that most hunters do not go to the woods to hunt, though that is the excuse they use to their spouses, bosses, bankers, and preachers. Same goes for fishing. We go to the woods and waters of this world to renew our spirits, to get away from the noise of automobiles or the ringing of telephones, to commune with Nature, to escape from the stresses of life in today's workplace, to dream the dreams of tomorrow, to regain our perspective of The One Who Made It All.

Venison stew or smoked turkey or fried bass filets are just icing on the cake, so to speak.

And in the final analysis, nowhere is our enjoyment of the outdoors so fulfilling as when we are sitting together with good friends around a campfire, listening to the owls, toasting old memories, and telling the stories of days gone by.

These are some of the best campfire stories you've ever been told. I am proud to be associated with these tellers.

Robert Hitt Neill

ACKNOWLEDGEMENTS

The Mississippi Wildlife Federation wishes to gratefully acknowledge the authors and artists and their representatives and publishers who have so willingly contributed their works for the causes of natural resource conservation, environmental quality, and outdoor recreation.

The Mississippi Wildlife Federation is an affiliate of the National Wildlife Federation, the world's largest private conservation organization. The objectives of the Federation are to create and encourage an awareness among the people of this nation for the need for the wise use and proper management of the earth upon which the lives and welfare of mankind depend—the soils, the waters, the forests, the minerals, the plantlife, and the wildlife.

QUIET RURAL SCENERY

Ernest Herndon

Ernest Herndon, McComb, is the Outdoors Editor for the **Enterprise-**Journal, *a free-lance writer, avid backpacker, canoer, and camper. He is also the award-winning author of several books including* Morning Morning True, In the Hearts of Wild Men, *and* Island Quarry.

Part of the trick to appreciating southwest Mississippi is to be observant. Although the area is rich in scenic beauty, it's not a dramatic beauty like glaciers, snow-capped mountains, or tumbling waterfalls. Instead, it's a landscape characterized by gently rolling hills, green pastures, gleaming ponds, and dark pine forests. Livestock brings the countryside to life as animals go about their business of living, be they horses grazing by a pond, a hog soaking nose-deep in a mudhole, or cattle lined up neck and neck at a feed trough. Fortunately for many of its peace-loving residents, southwest Mississippi has remained a little-known pocket of the country. Even many Mississippians are unaware of the drastic difference between the flat Mississippi Delta and the hilly, forested southwest corner. Although many non-resident urbanites have caught on to the exceptional hunting the area offers, so far this area has not become a tourist hotspot, though its pastoral beauty and historical heritage would recommend it. **Considering** what tourism has done to areas from Key West, Florida, to **Mendocino**, California, that might not be so bad. Rather, the area is probably most savored by its residents, especially those who appreciate detail. Detail, for instance, such as:

- The hazy quality of the air on an August afternoon over the shimmering pastures.

- The smell of new-mown hay as clippers and balers work their way across a broad field.

- The dense smell of pine trees, or the subtle scent of a cold-running stream.

- The sound of a lone mockingbird trilling in an oak tree.

- Children temporarily abandoning their high-tech toys for the simplest of pleasures, such as swinging from a vine or skipping pebbles in a pond.

- The thrash of a bass and hushed voices of fishermen as they try to land it.

- The sight of farmers loading ripe watermelons from field to pickup truck, and later of grinning children sprawled in a yard nose-deep in the bright red melon.

- An elderly woman, face shaded by straw hat, at work in her immaculate garden.

- A man in overalls working his pepper patch with a mule-drawn side harrow.

- An old wagon wheel, its faded red paint flaking off, leaning against the weathered boards of an abandoned barn.

- The hum of crickets and drone of bees over blackberry patches and dense thickets.

- The electrifying sight of a deer, its summer coat as red as rust, dancing up the side of a bank and disappearing into the woods.

- Or of a drove of wild turkeys, panicked, scatter-brained, and finally taking flight.

- The shrill of a hawk by daytime, the hoot of an owl by night.

- The antics of a pair of squirrels up and down an oak trunk.

- The pausing of a raccoon, eyes lit green by headlights, as it hustles off the road and into the bushes.

- The rustle and clatter on your porch which tells you a nosy opossum has come visiting again.

- The slight tang of boat motor fuel mixed with the smells of willows and water as you whisk through the cool air out across a lake.

- The smell of cornbread, peas, and fried chicken coming from the screened windows of a farmhouse.

- The taste of golden-fried catfish in early spring, fried okra and fresh tomatoes in the summer, and squirrel stew or barbecued deer meat in the fall.

- The sound of a fast, bourbon-colored stream running over sand and pebbles.

- The smell of gun oil on your favorite hunting piece, and the slightly mildewed scent of camouflaged clothes stored all summer long.

- The mist-choked sight of sunrise, cool on the hottest days, and later the red sun dropping like liquid onto the horizon.

- The moon rising through the pine trees, fat and yellow at first, then bright as silver when it clears the treetops and prompts the whippoorwill to call.

Southwest Mississippi doesn't have canyons, gorges, or mountain ranges. It doesn't need them.

DEATH IN THE CANEBRAKES

Jim McCafferty

Jim McCafferty, Ridgeland, is the Assistant Attorney General assigned to Mississippi Bureau of Pollution Control. He is a syndicated newspaper columnist and award-winning free-lance writer and photographer. He is the author of the forthcoming children's book Holt and the Teddy Bear..

Mississippi's Delta is a pretty tame-looking country today, a place of cotton fields, dusty turnrows, and long, straight highways. But about 100 years ago it was indeed a land of wonders. Back then it was called the Yazoo Delta for the river that ran through its heart, or simply "the swamp" or "the jungle."

By any name it was a most unusual land, almost tabletop flat and unrelieved by any but the slightest changes in elevation from Memphis to Vicksburg, the latter 200 miles south. As recently as the turn of the century the Delta was virtual wilderness, covered with some four million acres of bottomland hardwood forest, broken only by scattered towns and plantation villages. Deer and turkey filled the woods. Uncounted ducks, geese, and swans cruised its myriad lakes and bayous.

The Delta's first settlers were a breed of man like none today's generation has known. They must have been, for that fertile Eden was also a place of danger: of water moccasin and rattlesnake; of wolf and panther; of trackless swamp and confounding forest; of disastrous flood and malarial fever. It was, said one old settler, "a place where an alligator would die of consumption."

The very name Yazoo, in the Choctaw tongue, means "death." But for the hardy few who would brave mosquito and water moccasin, the Delta offered a chance for tremendous wealth in the form of cheap, fertile cotton land. The early cotton planters, wrote a correspondent for *Forest & Stream*, were particularly "fond of their guns, rods, dogs, and horses." Most of all, they loved bear hunting.

The Bear Hunters

The Delta pioneers hunted the black bear relentlessly, without regard for hour or season. In 1860, one Delta woodsman recorded 68 kills in five months. In 1869, another hunter's bag totaled 304—nine of which were taken in one day's hunt. As late as 1886, two Delta nimrods reported killing 30 bears in one summer.

"There are no society distinctions in the heart of the great swamps," wrote one Delta bear hunter. Men as diverse as the illiterate Holt Collier, born in bondage on a Mississippi plantation, and Confederate Gen. Wade Hampton III, perhaps the richest man in the antebellum South, hunted the bruin side by side. Rich or poor, slave or free, bear hunting was, as one anonymous bear hunter wrote in *Forest & Stream*, "the finest sport of all our hunting. Once you try it, it sticks, and the fondness for it will not shake or wear off."

Not all agreed with the assessment of the unidentified bear hunter. One veteran buffalo hunter confessed that an encounter with a Mississippi bear left him "scared all the way through," and more than a little adverse to again meeting a "bear on his native heather." Kit Dalton, a member of the notorious James Gang, recalled in his memoirs a time when Jesse James and "the boys" chanced onto a Delta bear hunt near Clarksdale. "It was our first experience in that kind of sport," he wrote, "and though we enjoyed listening to the yelping pack, there was little fun in trying to keep up with it through the terrible forests of cane and bamboo. We were scouts of many years' experience, but we had never encountered a Mississippi jungle before, and I will never tackle one of them again unless that were the sentence passed on me by the authorities for some of my misdeeds of the long ago."

Chasing a pack of bear hounds on horseback at a breakneck pace through morasses of cane, briar, and buckvine would seem to be danger enough for even the most foolhardy daredevil, but not for the most hard-bitten of the Yazoo bear hunters. For them, it was the knife, more than horse, hound, or jungle, that set the Delta style of bear hunting in a category all its own. "An expert did not shoot the bear," wrote one Delta scribe. "That was too crude. His purpose was to kill the animal by means of a knife held in his hand. If he failed with the knife, then he used the gun as a last resort."

The Bear

The Delta bear was no ordinary bruin, either. Because of the unsurpassed fertility of the Delta soil and the region's short, mild winters, these animals regularly reached tremendous sizes. Records from old magazine and newspaper articles indicate that 500- and 600-pounders were not particularly unusual. One gargantuan bruin killed near Clarksdale in 1869 reputedly strained the scales at 711 pounds—field dressed. No modern kill comes close to that unofficial record.

Even so, the typical Delta bear was rarely a threat to humans. Even a large bear, noted one hunter, would sooner fight its way through a pack of 20 dogs than face a single man. Yet when cornered or wounded, these Delta bears were, quite understandably, creatures with which to be reckoned. One early Delta hunter called his quarry "four to five hundred pounds of wild meat, a flask of powder, a score of rifle shots, and the salient argument of a bowie knife, before [it] is so eminently dead as to deserve an obituary notice."

Gen. Wade Hampton: The Mightiest of Bear Hunters

No doubt a few fearless backwoodsmen intentionally set out to conquer such beasts with steel instead of lead. General Hampton, whom Teddy Roosevelt called "with horse and hound the mightiest hunter America has ever seen," slew some 80 bears with the blade. And Ben Lilly— one of the last and greatest of the Delta bear-hunting breed—is reputed to have gone through a "knife phase" in his hunting career when he didn't even carry a firearm on his hunts. Far more often, though, situations, not personal tastes, dictated the use of the knife, as one Delta traveler learned when he spent a few days at Wildwood, General Hampton's Lake Washington plantation.

"If you are not familiar with bear," Hampton warned his guest prior to a bear hunt, "don't take him into close quarters. Put a ball through his heart before he can reach you with his paw; but if you fail to do this, stand not on the order of your going—leave!"

Not long into the hunt, the General wounded a big male. The pack hot on his heels, the old boar turned into the cane toward Hampton's companion. The guest raised his rifle and fired, missing the bear at what was little more than point-blank range. Gun empty, he turned and fled. The bear hesitated, took a few swats at the pack, and struck out after the fleeing hunter.

Fortunately, Hampton, who had been following the pack on foot, interceded. With one push of his powerful arm, the General shoved his frightened visitor far back into the cane. "Stay there as you value your life.

Don't move an inch," Hampton urged. In the direct path of the charging bruin, the General dropped to one knee and fired the first barrel of his 72 caliber double-barrel. The beast came on. As Hampton pulled the second trigger, a shoot of cane sprang from beneath his boot, knocking his shot awry. "In the twinkling of an eye," recalled Hampton's guest, "the General was on the ground, struck down by the forepaw of the enraged brute, but [with his] knife in hand, and as cool as if promenading his own piazza."

While the dogs harried the bear, Hampton, with the electric reflexes that would later save him at Gettysburg, reached from beneath that great, shaggy body and found the animal's heart. The bear turned toward the knife and collapsed. "The General recovered his feet without a scratch," the amazed narrator remembered, "gathered his gun, wiped the bloody knife in the dark fur, [and] sheathed it in an everyday sort of fashion."

The Bear Knife

The "bear knife" could be just about anything with a blade, from the giant machete-like cane-knife to the 9 $1/2$ inch-bladed "Arkansas Toothpick" used by Hampton. Col. R. E. Bobo, of Coahoma County used a Confederate bayonet. The single-edged bowie knife was the weapon of choice for many others. Others had their bear knives custom made. An 1843 outdoor magazine carried this detailed description of such a weapon:

"(The knife) will weigh two or three pounds—very much larger than the common bowie knife—about two-thirds the length of the Roman short sword, or the artillery sword, now in use. The instrument is generally of domestic manufacture, and is frequently made out of a large blacksmith's rasp that has been worn smooth; at least the rasp is preferred, if it can be had, in consequence of its superior temper. The handle is usually of buck's horn. The scabbard is made of sole leather, and is attached to the left side of the hunter by a strong belt of leather."

The Hunt

Even after repeating guns came along, the bear hunter's code of ethics sometimes necessitated resorting to steel. For example, the cardinal rule of honor among bear hunters was "Whatever you do, save the dogs"—not always a simple task given the bear dog's propensity to bite off more bruin than he could chew. The bear, one veteran Delta woodsman noted, further complicated the matter by "seek(ing) the heaviest canebrake for his battleground." Hunters almost always were forced to dismount and to pick, sometimes even cut, their way to the melee through virgin thickets of vine and cane. The delay could mean death to prized dogs, as turn-of-the century writer Harry Ball learned firsthand while hunting with his college friend, Delta planter Walter Morton.

Their quarry, a local, legendary bruin known as "the old She of Bayou Seche," had lured the hounds into "an impenetrable jungle of lapped and tangled growth twenty feet high, and spreading like a sea before us. We forced ourselves into (the cane), working, turning, and struggling, while Isom (Morton's dog handler) wielded his cane-knife in front of us to enlarge the way. Our progress was so slow that almost an hour was consumed before we came upon bear and dogs."

A grisly scene awaited. "No fewer than four of the dogs lay dead before her," Ball remembered, "and others were so covered with blood that their original color was indistinguishable." The old sow, already wounded by Morton's rifle, her back against a tree, "seemed literally to be covered with dogs, which had rushed anew to the attack as they saw us."

They fought the bruin so closely and savagely that, "It was impossible to shoot without further harming the already decimated pack." Anyway, said Ball, "Guns were useless in that almost impassable jungle. It was war to the knife, now." Isom drew his "cane-knife," which Ball described as "a dreadful weapon...formed of a broad iron blade about three feet long, with a short, stout handle." With a single swift, terrible stroke, he cleft the beast's shoulder to the bone. Almost at the same instant, "Walter rushed forward and plunged his hunting knife deep into the shaggy body." The wounds proved mortal, but not until a sweep of the old she-bear's paw had plowed inch-deep furrows in Morton's arm.

"It was not the first scratch that Walter had received from a bear's claws, however," concluded Ball, "and by the time we found our horses he was even laughing at the occurrence, and triumphing in the final conquest of his stout old foe."

The Dogs

Other times, the dogs carried the day. Mississippi writer James Gordon, in a classic tale of the Delta entitled "Bear Hunting in the Backwoods," recalled a hunt in which his pack saved his own bear-threatened life. Gordon had found the bear—again, an old sow with cubs—in open woods near a cane thicket, backed against a large tree, knocking dogs over "like nine-pins whenever they ventured too near." As Gordon closed in for the shot, "She started toward me with fierce, gleaming eyes and her red tongue lolling out like a fiery serpent, writhing in the white foam that dropped from her lips."

"A bear's head is a poor target," Gordon often said, "as it is in constant motion, and the frontal bones are so sharp and hard that unless the hunter makes a center shot, the ball will glance and do little harm." On this occasion, the Colonel forgot that bit of wisdom.

"I braced myself for a shot, and fired at her forehead," he wrote. The bear stumbled but rose in full charge. Gordon loosed a second shot, "and turned to run, when my foot caught in a bamboo vine and I fell. As I struggled to rise I turned, and she was on me!"

11

In desperation, Gordon jammed his rifle stock between the bear's powerful jaws. "I could hear the teeth grinding, as she crushed the wood in her iron jaws, with a sickening sensation, as I felt their next crunch would be my flesh and bones," he continued.

But all was not yet lost. "Old Lawyer, a grand bear dog I had often petted in camp, rushed to my rescue and seized the bear by the ear just as she wrenched the rifle from my hand and her grim lips touched my beard as she made a lunge for my throat. That noble dog," Gordon wrote, "with the strength and courage of a lion, realizing my danger, regardless of his own life, held on pulling at her ear with all his might.

"Take hold, dogs," Gordon shouted to the remainder of the pack, and take hold they did, covering the bruin and forcing her off their master. Freed from the weight of his would-be killer, Gordon unsheathed his bear knife and finished the fight.

Notable Bear Hunts

Such close encounters with death were not always devoid of humor—grim humor though it might have been. Ben Lilly, while hunting in the Little Sunflower wilderness of the southern Delta, once shot an oversized old he-bear. The beast went down, apparently dead. Lilly bent over to begin field dressing the animal, when the bear suddenly rose to its feet.

Lilly did the only thing he knew to do—he ran. The woods were open and the trees too big to climb. In desperation, he dashed around the biggest oak he could find, the bear in hot pursuit. For what seemed an eternity, Lilly and that bear chased each other's tails around that tree.

In what was in actuality only a half a minute or so later, but must have seemed an eternity, a terrified Lilly overtook and stumbled over his adversary. Fortunately, this time, the bear was actually dead.

Col. George Saunders, of Coahoma County, likewise got into trouble by prematurely pronouncing a bruin deceased. The Colonel stood astride his bear, preparing to cut its throat for bleeding, when the animal, without warning, took to its feet with Saunders on its back. The bear's resurrection so startled the Colonel that he dropped his knife and grabbed the animal's ears in an effort to keep it from biting him. The excitement of their master riding a bear was more than the dogs could stand. In one body they charged with jaws snapping, nipping the Colonel as often as the bear. Saunders shouted for help, but the scene was so outlandish that the Colonel's hunting partner, a fat, country preacher, was paralyzed with laughter. Finally the rest of the hunting party arrived and put the bear, Col. Saunders, and the parson out of their respective miseries.

Writing for *Scribner's Magazine*, Teddy Roosevelt once recounted the tale of a hunt that ended on a more tragic note. A Vicksburg man by the name of Leiser had crossed an unusually large bear track along the Big Sunflower River in the lower Delta. The size of it, in fact, had so unsettled Leiser that he had purposefully avoided the animal. "I never saw (a bear) that I was afraid to tackle," boasted Dr. Monroe Hamberlin, a well-known hunter of that day, on hearing the story. He gathered his hounds, his hunting gear, and a few companions and struck out for the Big Sunflower.

Hamberlin's dogs bayed the huge beast along Lake George near Satartia. Hamberlin reached them first and fired his muzzleloader at the bear's head. As so often happened, the ball glanced off the monster's sloping skull. The wounded, enraged bear charged and seized Hamberlin with its powerful jaws, stripping the flesh from the doctor's right thigh in the process.

Despite the incredible pain, Hamberlin managed to draw his knife. But before he could put it to work, the bear took hold again, this time snapping the doctor's arm like a tookpick. Hamberlin rallied his dogs, and they drove the bear off—but only momentarily. The bear attacked yet again with a bite to the base of the doctor's neck. Only the simultaneous arrival of another member of the party, who killed the bear with a single shot, prevented Hamberlin's immediate death. Though barely conscious, Hamberlin refused to leave without his opponent. The other hunters loaded the dead bear and the seriously wounded doctor into a skiff and floated downriver to Satartia. Dr. Hamberlin died three days later.

The bear weighed 640 pounds.

What drove men like Hamberlin and Lilly and Collier to purposefully place their lives in jeopardy, to depend for their very existence on their aim with a rifle or their speed with a bowie knife? "There is a fascination in danger that is inexpressible," Col. James Gordon once wrote in an attempt to explain that lust for the bear hunt. Even in his closest calls with *Ursae*, he confessed, he "felt a kind of joy in the situation."

The Yazoo Today

Colonel Gordon and the other members of the bear-hunting brotherhood would find little joy, little fascination, in most of today's Yazoo Delta. The clearing of the Delta's forests and the draining of its abundant wetlands began in earnest shortly after 1900. By 1940, William Faulkner, perhaps the greatest chronicler of the Delta's Big Woods, would write that the Delta had been "deswamped and derivered and denuded in two generations."

Still, a few isolated remnants of the timbered glory that was once the Delta have managed to survive (though even those are threatened by U.S. Army Corps of Engineers projects). In some of those areas, a handful of black bears hold on. The panther's cry, some say, is occasionally heard in those remote areas, and even an ivory-billed woodpecker is reportedly sighted from time to time.

14

If you can find one of these pieces of yesterday, and if you know the old stories, it's not too hard to imagine that old country, even though you never knew it yourself—that country of dark woods and quiet waters, where wolf and panther prowled, that country where bear, dog, man, and his knife kept their rendezvous with death in the canebrakes.

Shade Steele

GASTROINTESTINAL RUMBLINGS

Jim Ritchie

Jim Ritchie, Canton, owns The Computer Results Company and is a part-time writer and storyteller. He is also author of the forthcoming book I Think God Loves Me Anyway.

I 'm no cook. My culinary capability consists of an average ability to smear mayonnaise on two pieces of bread and plop a slice of bologna (or is it baloney?) on one mayonnaise-smeared side and gently place the other piece of bread on top. Occasionally when I pat the top bread slice in place, I discover that the mayonnaised side is face up. Then I carefully turn the top bread slice over and wash my hand.

I can make a pretty good bowl of popcorn if I have at my disposal the old pot part of a pressure cooker which I rescued for this purpose when my better half threw it away. I also foraged around and found a near-fitting pot lid to complete the ensemble, which now sits by the stove at all times. I've tried to wash the pot once or twice, but the grease drippings down the side of the pot from years of popping wouldn't wash, chip, or scour off, so I quit worrying about it. She just hides it now when company comes. I can also scramble an egg, and that usually works out OK if I put enough chopped-real-fine onion in it. Other than these three items, any food ingredient that I touch fire or boiling water to will generally turn into something that would give a buzzard colic.

I sometimes dream of preparing a sure enough big-league candlelight dinner of fricasseed something-or-other replete with tender rice and vegetables and good wine all hot at the same time. Except the wine. Then when the folks ooh and aah about how good it is, I could sit back with just a hint of a smile and fend off compliments, like most good cooks do.

My mother, who is one of the best cooks in at least the world, fends off compliments.

"Ma, these biscuits are *outstanding!*"

Does she say, "Thanks. And wasn't that squash casserole simply scrumptious?" She does not. She says, "I should have left those biscuits in the oven for just another minute. Then they would have browned prettier. Another pinch of salt wouldn't have hurt, either."

She knows very well that one more minute in the oven *would* have been too long, and that another pinch of salt *would* have hurt. Beats me.

When I was little, we had a maid named Esther Williams (*not* the swimming movie star). She was remarkably, extraordinarily, uncommonly wonderful. I loved her. Esther showed up every morning in her starched white uniform dress ready to handle any situation or chore in her unhurried, competent manner, whether it was housecleaning, playing cowboys and Indians, paddling my rear if I needed it, or any of the dozens of other things she was called on to do. But where she really excelled was in the kitchen. And when she and my mother got together on the serious preparation of a meal, the stuff they put on the table was sinful. Anything that good had to be sinful.

She didn't use recipes. She just kind of felt her way along, and I don't remember a single failure. One time Mama asked Esther for her recipe on molasses cookies, which were the envy of the neighborhood. Esther said, "You takes a couple of doublehandfuls of flour, two pinches of salt, etc., etc., and kneads it all together 'til it looks right. Then add three gullops of molasses and knead it again, then pinch off the cookies and put them in the oven 'til they're ready." Mama said, "Esther, I understand all of it but the gullops of molasses. What in the world is a *gullop*?"

"Aw, Miss Bobbie. You just throws the jug of molasses over your arm and pour. It says 'Gullop, Gullop, Gullop,' and you cuts it off." *Man*, she could cook!

I've noticed something about cooking, though. Food prepared outside and eaten outside is generally passable if not downright delicious when the same stuff cooked and consumed inside would gag a maggot. I'm not talking about a backyard barbeque. That's usually done too close to the house. I'm talking about vittles created in the woods and wolfed down after a hard day's hunt. I've smelled dog food mixed with hot water in that setting that got my head close enough to the pan to where the dogs growled at me. I don't think I would have eaten any even if the dogs hadn't growled, but it sure smelled good.

The only times I didn't like outside food was when I was in the Army. But somehow that shouldn't count. I was *told* to eat outside there, by God. And the cuisine wasn't anything to write home about. We had K rations and C rations most of the time in the field. If "A" stands for excellent and "F" stands for failure in grading systems, they had those rations marked "K" graded about right. In the early 60's, I got a box of K rations with a pack of Lucky Strike cigarettes in it that had a *green* wrapper. I understand that "Lucky Strike Green Goes To War!" was a familiar slogan once. But the war they were talking about was World War II, folks. These rations I was eating had to be plus or minus twenty years old. I got to worrying about eating twenty-year-old meat. Not to worry, I was told. They preserved that stuff with something akin to embalming fluid, and that, I was told, would keep the meat from rotting for eons. After I gained that information, I traded meat for peaches and crackers. I don't know whether the embalming fluid bit was true, but nothing in an olive drab can tasted the same afterwards. I didn't reckon that peaches or crackers had to be embalmed.

I'd be less than honest if I didn't mention the only time I can remember (outside of the Army) when a woods-cooked meal was absolutely inedible. My father cooked it. He wasn't used to cooking. We had my mother, you see, as I mentioned before.

On this particular occasion, my mother's brother, Uncle Johnny, my dad, my little brother (also Johnny), and I went on an all-night catfishing trip to the Bogue Chitto River around Brookhaven, Mississippi. We set out lines in the afternoon and ran them all night. To no avail. It was like the catfish had lockjaw that night. "*But*," my dad said, "just wait 'til I fix your breakfast! I'm gonna make you forget that we didn't catch any fish." He was right. He had brought some eggs, ham steak, and grits and planned to make "redeye" gravy out of the ham and river water. It was worse than awful. I still can't exactly figure what went wrong to make all of it taste sort of dirty metallic. My brother and I (we were 8 and 10 at the time) kind of picked around the edges, hoping against hope that the old "clean your plate" order wouldn't be voiced. Uncle Johnny saved us. He looked my dad straight in the eye and said, "Red, if Bobbie set something like this in front of you, there wouldn't be a judge in the world who wouldn't let you off if you beat the hell out of her." To his credit, and to our relief, my dad said, "You're right." And we loaded everything up and went to a cafe for breakfast.

I have on occasion found out, however, that just because something cooked at a camp is palatable, it isn't necessarily good *for* you. My bird dog and I were invited by Joe Hand to go on a Texas quail hunt one time down around San Antonio. (The dog was actually invited. They had to carry me because it was my dog.) The first morning there, I started scrambling the eggs with the chopped-real-fine onions in them. The fellow who was hosting us took a keen interest in my preparation and found it

19

was less than adequate. "Hell, boy, let me show you how we fix eggs in west Texas." Ground-up chili peppers, sloshed all over with Tabasco sauce and God knows what else, were stirred into the eggs, and the resulting concoction was finally up to his standards after much tasting and addition of more chili peppers and Tabasco. After the first bite, and everything from the lips to the stomach was cauterized, they tasted pretty good. Those eggs stayed with me all day. And all through the next night. I was trying to sleep, and those eggs were doing battle with whatever they could find to do battle with. My stomach sounded like a championship dog fight. Even if the queasy feeling hadn't been considered, the noise would have kept me awake. The next morning, I could have bowed up and put those eggs through a keyhole at twenty feet. I mean the water in the toilet was absolutely whitecapping. And I discovered that the cauterizing effect didn't stop with the stomach. I made a mental note not to eat any more Texas-style eggs.

The best outside meal I ever ate will never be exactly duplicated. It won't be duplicated for the simple reason that nobody knows exactly what went into it. It was a pure community project with contributions from everyone who wished to participate. It didn't start out that way, but that's the way it turned out. And it was, as the saying goes, indescribably delicious.

We were at deer camp, and somebody decided that we should scour out the old wash pot that had been sitting in the middle of camp for years and which nobody could find a good use for, since things are not usually washed at deer camp. Clothes or people. Then, once the pot was relatively free of the mysterious residue which had accumulated on it, we could make a stew. Some of us thought that was a good idea (that night, after all the toasts to the deer, dogs, outdoor life, rifles, shotguns, and the Methodist Church, among other things, *anything* would have been a good idea), so we bustled around and hit the pot a few licks with some SOS pads to make it presentable. Maybe not presentable to the Pure Food and Drug Act folks, but it looked OK to us. Willie, the camp helper, did most of the work, since he had not participated too heavy in the toasting session.

We filled the pot about half full of water, built a fire around it, and, when the water boiled, we began the scientific act of adding the ingredients. Some potatoes went in, along with canned tomatoes, lots of salt and pepper, some of last year's celery salt that somebody's wife had brought to camp on a fishing trip the previous summer, and other things like that. We added a few pounds of deer meat, a squirrel or two, a duck or two, a couple of what was purported to be quail, and other things like *that*. Then we made sure that we had enough wood stacked around the pot to last the night, and went to bed.

The next morning, before we took up stands, we checked the stew, and it was doing fine. One of the pseudo cooks, who had been one of the main toasters the night before, and who had at least temporarily sworn off toasting, poured a fifth of Jack Daniels Black Label in "to give it a little twang." A couple of real dyed-in-the-wool hunters, who passed on the toasting session, and who had killed a coon and a possum the night before, added these prizes to the stew that morning. Then we stacked enough wood around the pot to last the morning and went deer hunting.

We came in around noon to rest up and get ready for the afternoon hunt, and to check on the stew. It was still roiling and boiling and doing great. After a test or two by a bunch of folks, we began to fine tune the taste. Some onions, hot sauce, a rabbit, meat tenderizer, and a few more twang ingredients were added. The stew had boiled down to where everything in it was pretty nondescript in a sort of mush. The bubbles that pushed up through all that stuff popped in a kind of meaty "blup." A statement was made that somebody could fall in *that* stew and be forever unaccounted for. Then somebody hollered for Willie to fetch some more wood. No Willie. That was not like him: not to be around when you needed him. The thought occurred to all of us at the same time that Willie was "unaccounted for." All eyes went to the stew.

"Blup....blup."

Nobody said anything, but we all dispersed in a hell of a hurry to look for Willie, and, happily, somebody found him asleep over by the skinning rack. A piece of wire mesh from the dog pen area was hurriedly put over the pot to satisfy any OSHA requirements, and we stacked enough wood around the pot to keep it going through the afternoon, and went back to the woods.

After we returned from the afternoon hunt, tired, cold, wet from a light all-afternoon drizzle, and hungry enough to eat the hind end out of a rag doll, we decided that the stew was ready, and we ate it. All of it. And if I had the exact recipe for that stew, my balance sheet would look better than General Motors'. I have eaten in some multi-star restaurants all over the country, but I have never tasted anything that even remotely could measure up to that. I mean it was *outstanding*. And it gets better as the years go by.

My belly doctor told me shortly thereafter that I had an ulcer. But I'm not blaming the stew. Nothing that good could cause an ulcer.

NOXUBEE MEMORIES

Billy Ellis

Billy Ellis, Lexington, is Board Chairman of Holmes County Bank. An expert bowhunter, he has taken 30 different big-game species—many of which are listed in the Pope & Young, Boone & Crockett, or Safari Club International records. He is Trust Officer for Pope & Young Club, a freelance writer, and award-winning author of Hunter to the Dawn.

T he rooster crowed, the jackass brayed, and old Snaps, the pointer, bumped his rheumatoid backbone on the undercarriage of the creaking country house. It was a golden dawn in Noxubee County, Mississippi. The early-morning light refracted through the greying lead-glass panes, and now darkly through the misty memory of a grown man—then a tousled-headed city boy with a chunk of joy in his throat and the world before him.

I pulled on my clothes and made my way through the rambling, labyrinthine country house, out the never-locked back door, and onto the tin-roofed walkway to the old kitchen, which stood ten yards out back. I shivered in the morning cold until I pushed open the weather-beaten kitchen door. The heat inside warmed my body as well as my spirit. Granky, my Wilkins grandmother, held sway over the great wood stove, and her sons, recently spared from the Axis hordes, swilled great cups of strong coffee from ancient stoneware mugs. That smell of hickory smoke, coffee, and thick slabs of home-cured bacon is still fresh after forty years.

Once an old Eskimo woman, sick and depressed in a far and strange land, told her nurse, "Sometimes I raise my hands before my eyes and stare at them; right in my own hands I can see the shorelines, beaches, lakes, and mountains where I came from." In my heart's eye, when I see Granky's hands— plump, white, dishwater hands—kneading the dough, I remember where I came from. Those hands were once artist's hands at Mississippi State College for Women so very long ago, but she had given up art for a loftier and higher form of sculpture: kneading love into the dough.

The menfolk made plans for the day's hunt over an incredibly fine breakfast of grits, scrambled eggs, thick slabs of bacon, cat-head biscuits, and homemade fig preserves from the old fig tree behind the smokehouse. Thank goodness no one had yet discovered cholesterol, triglycerides, or carcinogens! We were in the best of times. Granky's boys were safe, and the world had a vibrancy and brilliance that only children can really feel.

The guineas were just starting their raucous cackling when Granddaddy Tyson Wilkins took me in tow. He and I would hunt the Back Forty. Old liver-marked Snaps ran by the smokehouse and headed out to "Quail Country." Granddaddy slipped three shells into his old beat-up Browning Sweet Sixteen, and we moved out past squealing pigs, pump house, horse barn, rusting harrows, and other extraneous refuse that always surrounds an old country homestead. The sun was just up, and a thin fog still blanketed the gently rolling prairie hills. "Hup, Snaps!" Granddaddy called. The old pointer slowed and started to work, ranging back and forth, a flicker of white in and out of the patches of ground fog in the surreal early morning landscape. Then the white dot was stationary.

"He's got 'em!" whispered Granddaddy as I ran after him, panting and expectant, but not really knowing quite what to expect. He handed me the shotgun and whispered, "Shoot a bird, not the covey." I have never felt such responsibility except the time I shivered expectantly in a tiny church by the Mississippi River and said, "I do."

24

Snaps had worked in tight on the covey in a perfect point. My heart was in overdrive. The sage crunched underfoot while I found the safety. "Walk past him," whispered Granddaddy.

An explosion occurred and the buff bombshells rocketed out of the sage. I swung on the whole covey. Gun blast, kick, and no bird fell. I forgot to shoot again.

"We'll get the singles," promised Granddaddy. He then showed me how; with the pointer holding pretty, a single thundered up from underfoot, to explode in a shower of feathers. Old Snaps dutifully brought back each one, mouthing them gently, and we soon had six birds. Granddaddy called a rest break about noon.

We stopped at an old falling-down dogtrot house. The old man pulled a couple of roast beef sandwiches out of his hunting coat. "I'm feeling my seventy-four years," he confessed. "Let's sit here on the porch, and while we're here, I guess this is as good a time as any to tell you what tired really is and what courage is all about.

"My daddy, your great-granddaddy, had this farm and left me the big house. Some day in school, you'll learn in the history books about General Robert E. Lee and the Army of Northern Virginia. I don't know everything there is to know about all the battles, but I do know that Daddy was in our local company, the Prairie Guards, Company E of the Eleventh Mississippi Regiment in Lee's army. They were one of the first companies to volunteer, and since General Grant wasn't even a general then, much less raising havoc in Mississippi, Daddy's regiment was shipped to Virginia and fought under Lee for the whole war.

"He went through every battle that Lee fought, and was wounded seven times. It takes a heap of courage and a lot of love for your homeland to keep going when you're hurt, tired, sick, hungry, and thirsty most of the time. Both of his brothers, Henry Clay Wilkins and Davy Crockett Wilkins, were killed, one on either side of him, when they went up the hill in

Pickett's Charge at Gettysburg. Out of the thirty-seven men in their company, only one man was able to answer roll call back down at the bottom of Cemetery Ridge that evening. Only one man, boy! I know folks in almost every house around here that grieved for a lost boy or two.

"Son, all day you've been complaining. Tired, thirsty, or something. I want you to remember what I just told you. Those boys went up that hill regardless of politics or ideology; they went up as simple country boys. They were defending what they perceived was right, protecting their homes and families, and they persevered through untold suffering.

"Right after Gettysburg, Daddy fought all the way back to Hatcher's Run right before Appomattox. By then, our troops were pitiful skeleton boys with no shoes and tattered, threadbare uniforms. They were starving and sick, but they still had that bright glint of bravery and total, even mystical, commitment in their eyes.

"On the last night, they were completely surrounded by the Yankees, and Lee's army was pushed up against a creek called Hatcher's Run. Just as the sun was setting for the last time on the greatest army the world has ever known, a long, rolling, shrill cry welled up. Starting three miles up Hatcher's run and rolling down the Confederate lines, the Rebel Yell rolled like thunder down the creek, telling Grant that those lines were welded in a love that transcends any human comprehension.

"The next day, that bunch of pitiful scarecrow-boys was thrown into line. The tattered Stars and Bars flag fluttered before each regiment, only a few yards apart because each one had been decimated down to mere company size. General Lee and General Gordon rode the line, tears flowing down their cheeks. They knew the end was near, not just for the army, but for a way of life.

"General John B. Gordon stopped his prancing bay in front of a pitiful Confederate soldier. Both of his arms had been almost shot away, and they dangled helplessly at his sides. 'Get to the aid station, sir,' the general ordered. 'You cannot go into combat in your condition.'

"'I know I can't fight, sir,' the soldier replied, 'but I can still yell!'"

"'I CAN STILL YELL!'"

Lord, how I remembered that story. When the path grows dim, when the trail gets too rough, when the world closes in, I think of that pitiful, starving boy in homespun gray with the glint in his steel-blue eyes and a love that transcends all understanding in his heart.

Granddaddy pulled out an old, yellowed clipping from his pocket and handed it to me. "I thought you would like to have your great-granddaddy's eulogy, which was written by his commanding officer, Captain A. J. Ervin."

I started to read:

"Eulogy of Thomas J. Wilkins, Co. E, 11th Mississippi Regiment:....he was gallant and dependable in battle, and in camp and on the march he was always joyous and happy; never a cloud, however threatening, but that he could see the sunshine beyond. His most marked characteristic, however, was his intense and active interest in a sick or wounded comrade. No march could be so disagreeable and so protracted, no weather so severe as to prohibit his spending the night in a vigil by the pallet of a sick or suffering comrade; and he was one of the few who seemed to enjoy battling with death—in comforting where he could not cure, in soothing where he could not save."

Granddaddy and I left the old dogtrot house and walked back toward the big house. I didn't feel like hunting any more that day, and old Snaps seemed to sense it as he ambled along at our feet all the way back to the house.

* * * *

That was many years ago. The old house, called Sunnyside, is gone, a victim of the vicissitudes of time and the cold, impersonal scalpel of a bulldozer blade. It's all gone—my tree house, the old smokehouse, the warm old kitchen, the feather beds, the old folks, the love and dreams that chink the walls of a country home. I go back occasionally, when the Lord calls another family soul back to the limestone clay of Noxubee County. As the preacher intones, "Dust unto dust, and to the dust returneth," my eyes stray to the large granite marker in our family plot. The inscription simply reads "T. J. Wilkins, Co. E, 11th Mississippi."

Bravery and love are all the consolation we need.

Shade Steele

MISSISSIPPI'S FAVORITE FISH

Jim Robbins

Jim Robbins, Tunica, is a Fish & Wildlife Biologist with the Corps of Engineers. He is a free-lance writer and author of the forthcoming book - Crappie!

T he school of crappie suspended lethargically in 12 feet of water in an open expanse of the willow-lined river chute, a former bed of the mighty Mississippi, but now cut off from "Ole Miss" by earthen plugs on both ends that had slowly filled in over the decades. Only during winter and spring floods did the big river add her invigorating influx.

Twice during the coldness of February—and it had been severe by lower Mississippi Valley standards—the school had migrated downstream to the runout leading to the river, but they had returned to their winter holding area in the mouth of one of the three creeks feeding the oxbow.

This was the fourth winter for the school, which numbered perhaps 100 fish of one to two pounds. Their efforts to spawn the past two springs had been unsuccessful due to high waters which had receded before the eggs hatched and left them dry. The gap in the standing crop would soon be noticed by fishermen.

The short February days were becoming not noticeably longer, but longer. The sun became a direct influence on the movements of the school. When a characteristic warm spell occured in mid-month, accompanied by three days of sunshine, the school shallowed up just below the surface.

The new warmth seemed to stimulate other creatures—a five-foot alligator gar swept through the tightly bunched school and injured two of the panfish before grasping a victim in toothed jaws. His demeanor and physique hadn't changed since prehistoric times.

No less a predator than the fearsome gar, but one that had been absent for many years in the Mississippi river bottoms, suddenly appeared and scattered the school again, taking one of the smaller males for a shoreline banquet—a river otter. Yet another member was lost to an aerial strike from a bald eagle—a former resident of the Mississippi Valley which, like the otter, had in recent years returned in sufficient numbers to add an unforgettable splendor to the wildness of the river bottoms. The eagle and his mate had migrated from Canada, following the concentrations of waterfowl down the flyway, preying primarily on weak or crippled ducks. But he couldn't resist an easy fish dinner when he saw the school sunning near the surface. The fish the raptor selected was bigger than anticipated, and he had to exert a great deal of energy to lift the two-pounder back to his dead snag.

These predations, though disrupting, were natural, and the school would persist in spite of them if other disasters could be averted, such as farm chemical pollution or a third straight year of lost spawn. It would take years to rebuild the oxbow back to its former productivity.

A cold front sent the crappie deeper, but urges were stirring that had been long dormant. Winter was wearing down. The school became more restive and scattered. They sensed that changes were imminent. A warm rain the first of March provided the stimulus that they had been waiting for; a second, heavier rain, followed by a third, sent the rising chute into new ground as it spread through the flat bottomlands and over beaver dams into nearby corn and soybean fields.

After three days of high water, the school, which had remained loosely intact, left the deep water safety of the tributary to scatter and prowl for food in the inundated territory. For a week, they fed on crustaceans, minnows, and aquatic insects and then began to search for spawning sites. Water temperatures were warming fast.

A fortuitous fall in the flood crest the next day prevented a reoccurrence of the last two years, at least for the present. Able to sense the slightest change in water levels, the crappie began moving back to drainage ditches and sloughs. Natural obstructions to the receding waters such as duck blinds, beaver dams, and log jams, became prime feeding stations for the voracious panfish who waited in ambush in the eddies. One obstruction threatened the entire school when a fast-falling river almost marooned them behind a beaver dam. Only a small rivulet near the center was deep enough for them to ford the barrier. A number of large carp were also stranded, and they were helping keep the gap open by flapping their heavy bodies across one by one. The thrashing of scales and tails attracted an interested spectator who quickly decided to join in the fun—a raccoon. He grasped and wrestled three or four giant carp to no avail and much to his disappointment when his dexterous paws wrapped around one of the smaller crappies. With experience borne of working under the water for frogs and crawfish, he flipped the fish onto the beaver dam where it was finally dispatched.

As "Ole Miss" withdrew, so did the crappie—back into their tributary. Downstream, the migrating fish encountered another obstacle—one more formidable this time, as the illegal size meshes of a fish poacher's net stretched across the mouth of the narrow creek captured the big crappie by the dozens. A number of them jumped instinctively over the top to safety. Only about half of the school that had started the winter was left.

By the last of March, the oxbow stabilized for the time being and the school dispersed into the shallows to spawn around cypress knees, fallen logs, brush, duck blinds, and treetops. Snapping turtles, anchored in the mud in brushpiles, picked off an easy meal from time to time before the females returned to deeper water. Spawning was successful. Stable water conditions produced a bumper crop of fry—enough to withstand the rigors of predation and natural disasters and to provide a productive base for succeeding generations.

This scene is replayed every year in all of the old chutes, sloughs, and oxbows connected to the Mississippi River from Memphis to Pinckneyville.

It is also replayed in all other types of crappie waters in different degrees. A crappie in Ontario's Lake of the Woods or Chautauqua Lake in New York may not have to fend off an alligator gar but he does have to occasionally dodge a muskie or northern pike! And while a crappie in southwest lakes may not face any of these predators, he still stands to lose his life in the jaws of a striped bass or largemouth bass! In fact, the introduction of striped bass into Nevada's Lake Mead and Lake Mohave has spelled doom for these once fertile crappie waters.

The poor crappie is comparable to the lowly rabbit......everybody wants to eat him for dinner. And they do. It's a wonder of nature that any survive, especially considering the inroads man makes on their populations. More noble gamefish (bass, trout, pike, muskie) all have their devotees who release those that are caught. Do crappie fishermen practice catch & release? The obvious answer is no, because I had never seen anybody release a crappie until recently. And believe it or not, the practice can be beneficial to the fishery. Perhaps the most important benefit comes during the spring spawning season. Depending on body weight, a female crappie, either black or white, may deposit 7,000 to 200,000 eggs in a sand or gravel nest fanned out by the male black crappie or on roots and limbs of bushes and trees in the case of white crappie.

After egg-laying, the female departs, leaving the parental chores to the male, who must fan the eggs to insure their hatching. Remove the male, and the eggs will either be covered with destructive fungus or eaten by small fish. The male is the key to a successful spawn. Therefore, when fishing during the traditional spawning season when you know or feel sure crappie have spawned, return the males to their nest-guarding duties and seek out the females in deeper water.

Just who is this fish we call a crappie? Actually, not everybody calls him a crappie. The Fish Nomenclature Committee of the Outdoor Writers Association of America spearheaded a movement a few years ago to adopt an approved list of common names for North American sport fish. Homer Circle, the chairman of that committee, admitted that it wasn't easy because there were 55 common names for the crappie being used across America! I won't list all 55 names, but in the Deep South, "white perch" is fairly common, while in Florida the name "specks" is popular statewide, and in Louisiana, the Cajun word "sac-a-lait" is used, which means bag of milk, a tribute to its delicate meat and table quality.

Bob Dennie, Editor of *The Louisiana Conservationist*, tells an interesting story of the largest crappie ever caught in Louisiana, or for that matter, the world! In November of 1969, Littie Robertson was fishing from the bank of the Westwego Canal when she hooked and landed a crappie which was photographed and then weighed on certified scales at six pounds! A new world mark that would best either of the two current record-holders in the black crappie or white crappie categories.

Littie, glad when all the uproar over the catch was finally over, took the fish home and ate it for supper......the same fate suffered by the world-record walleye and largemouth bass. And no doubt by other species whose captors didn't realize what they had caught.

However, Littie's crappie suffered a worse fate. The photograph could not reveal whether the fish was a white or a black crappie, and since no bonafide authority had viewed the remains, it could not be recognized as a new world record for either species.

The state of Louisiana didn't understand why there was so much fuss about whether it was black or white—they listed it as the state record sac-a-lait!

Consult any scientific description of the two species of crappie and you'll find both fish are physically the same, with one obvious difference besides coloration. The white crappie (*Pomoxis annularis*) has six spines on the dorsal fin and the black (*Pomoxis nigromaculatus*) has seven or eight. Their scientific names give a clue to the difference in coloration. *Pomoxis* is a Greek word meaning "opercle sharp"...obviously not giving a clue to coloration, but the species name does—*annularis* is a Latin word meaning "having rings" and refers to the dark bands or "bars" on the body. *Nigromaculatus* is also Latin and means "black spotted", a reference to an all-over pattern of irregularly arranged speckles and blotches.

Mississippi at present holds the world record for white crappie—a five-pound three-ounce specimen caught in Enid Reservoir by Fred L. Bright of Memphis. The fish was taken in the middle of the summer (July 31, 1957) and might have weighed over six pounds had she been caught before spawning. The biggest black crappie of record is a four-pound eight-ouncer caught on March 1, 1981, in Kerr Lake, which straddles the Virginia/North Carolina border.

So, the next time you haul in a slab crappie, take a moment and reflect on the number of potential predators and pitfalls it may have gone through before engulfing your minnow or jig......the crappie is worthy of respect.

THE CABLE BRIDGE GOBBLER

David Rainer

David Rainer, Brandon, is a staff writer and photographer for The Jackson Clarion-Ledger. *He is also a frequent free-lance writer for several magazines.*

I suppose bruised egos get more people in binds than just about anything. I know I've let my mouth overload my not-so-dainty derriere more than once. Having hunted wild game in Mississippi since I was old enough to fire a shotgun and still be standing up afterward, I've had my share of blown shots. However, for my first 36 years, none of those misses involved turkeys, I'm sure, because I'd never hunted them.

"You mean you've lived in Mississippi all your life and you've never killed a turkey?" said one guy from Missouri, who had come to Mississippi just to hunt the Eastern subspecies.

"But the crappie are spawning in the spring," I responded in sort of hangdog fashion, trying to avoid eye contact.

"You mean you're an outdoor writer and you've never killed a turkey?" he said, salting the wound.

"But the bass are..."

Actually, when I was growing up in the northeast part of the state, seeing a wild turkey was almost unheard of. I had never experienced the thrill of that particular hunting, so I didn't realize what I was missing. I probably still wouldn't know had my ego not been thoroughly assaulted.

35

Since pride means so much to us Southerners, I had no choice but to pursue what I would learn was a clever foe.

My first two hunts were inconsequential, but the third changed me from a determined turkey hunter to a desperate turkey hunter. Because of my inexperience, I wasn't positioned properly in a blind on the edge of a huge pasture. At dawn, the field filled with turkeys. Instead of coming straight to the calling, they circled to my right. I soon found out a normal shot for a right-handed shooter was out of the question. As the birds circled, I ever-so-slowly switched the gun to my left shoulder. Undoubtedly, a longbeard gobbler detected the movement and high-tailed it back out of range. But a jake, as inexperienced as I was at this turkey hunting game, stood there with his neck stretched out, trying to figure out why in the heck the big gobbler departed.

The awkwardness was apparent as I hunkered down on the barrel with the shotgun on my left shoulder. But I figured this jake was as good as in the roasting pan when I pulled the trigger. The blast that echoed across the field was soon drowned out by flapping turkey wings against the cool morning air. It was a cold, clean miss. To make matters much worse, it was all on video-tape. If you've never experienced an humbling incident like that, you cannot imagine the amount of grief that can be dished out by your hunting companions.

"We're sorry we called the turkeys up on the wrong side," deadpanned Jack Wood and Zac Whaley, the expert turkey callers positioned about 20 yards behind the blind.

"The next time, just wait until we call the gobbler into the blind and then you can grab him and wring his neck."

After about six hours of ragging, I knew this incident would undoubtedly be with me on my deathbed. I figured the only way I would ever get a moment's peace would be to kill a quality bird. Hence, I hunted with a passion through the season, to no avail. I saw turkeys and heard turkeys, but I didn't get a shot at vindication. I'd put up with chiggers, ticks, mosquitoes, and a numb behind and had nothing to show for it except insect bites.

I was down to my last hunt. I let two hours of sleep suffice before I headed for West Point for a rendezvous with Bill Sugg, a Senior Vice President with Haas Outdoors, makers of Mossy Oak camouflage. Sugg had asked me the night before if I could handle crossing a cable bridge, although he offered no details. I responded, with tongue-not-too-firmly-planted-in-cheek that "I was BIG, but agile." There, I'd done it again with my alligator mouth.

The words "cable bridge" conjure up different mental images for different folks, I suppose. When I heard the words, my mind pictured a bridge made up of three strands of cable in a triangular pattern. the bottom strand is used to stand on and the other two cables are about mid-torso high. Some type of rope is used to connect the two top cables to the bottom one for stability. It's the kind of apparatus any normal six-year-old could traverse with relative ease.

However, my mental image and reality were not even close when I walked up to Chuquatonchee Creek with Sugg. I should have known this was not going to be an easy hunt when Sugg saw me pull my Browning pump out of the gun case. My gun didn't have a sling.

"You better take my gun," he said. "I don't think you'll ever get across the bridge trying to hold a gun."

After a 200-yard walk down to the creek, I suddenly realized why. In the dim light of the slowly emerging dawn was "the cable bridge." There were two creosote poles guyed to the ground and two, count them, two strands of cable stretched across the creek. And, there was nothing stringing the two cables together. Had it not been for the fact that I had to kill a turkey just to be able to show my face in Claiborne County, I might have turned tail and run, much like the aforementioned longbeard. But I was determined not to pass up any chance at killing a turkey, even if it meant taking a creek-water bath.

The long-legged Sugg climbed up on the bridge and started across. With the top strand tucked under his right arm, Sugg slid down the cable. I was beginning to feel a little better about my chances until he got to the bottom of the swag. All of a sudden the cable started to sway, and Sugg held on for dear life. Finally, the swaying settled back down and he made it across.

I figured I was wet for sure, but I climbed up and hooked my arches on the cable and took a death grip on the top strand. I slid along, inches at a time. Going down the swag was not too bad, but when I reached the bottom, it was almost like some invisible prankster had grabbed the cable and started to shake it.

My feet went one way and then the other. The cable dug into my arm pit, but I managed to hang on. I was determined to keep my arches hooked on the bottom cable, and I silently thanked Mr. L. L. Bean for putting those steel shanks in my boots. I managed to slide a few feet before the prankster struck again. My body was undulating like a belly dancer, trying to keep up with the whims of the cable. Finally, Sugg grabbed the top strand to slow down the swaying, and I struggled the last few feet to the opposite side of the creek. I hopped down off the bridge, out of breath, but still mostly dry.

"I wasn't worried," Sugg said later. "I knew if he fell in that he'd be out in a hurry if he heard a turkey gobble."

About an hour later I would be out of breath again. Not from physical exertion, but from the kind of excitement that makes turkey hunting so addictive.

A half mile from the creek, we heard a gobble. We picked up the pace as the gobble got louder and louder. Finally, Sugg decided we were close enough, so we set up by a huge oak.

I had been forewarned that the mosquitoes were particularly bad in this creek bottom, so I had sprayed myself with insect repellent before we went into the woods. I was standing up at the time and didn't realize I had missed a couple of spots. When we sat down by the tree, those spots were exposed—the insides of my thighs. Mosquitoes were buzzing around my head for a moment, until they swarmed to my unprotected legs. I tried to keep from squirming because I was too close to soothing my mental anguish.

Sugg had slipped a diaphragm call in his mouth and was making soft yelps. The gobbler was very much interested in what he was saying, and there was no doubt the bird was headed our way. There was a patch of thick undergrowth in front of us preventing us from seeing the approaching gobbler. Sugg's calling became a little more aggressive, and I soon realized why. A hen was in the area and Sugg had some tough competition. Momentarily Sugg won out. He figured the bird would circle one way or the other. I had the gun to my shoulder, ready to swing one way or the other, when directly behind us came a "Putt, purrrrrrr. Putt, purrrrrrr. Putt, purrrrrrrr." We'd been flanked by a jake, and his alarm calls made our gobbler do an about-face.

"If you see that damned jake, blow his head off," Sugg said. But I had no shot, and as it turned out, I'm thankful I didn't.

"Oh well, that's the most action I've had in a while," I told Sugg as I grabbed the insect repellent and soaked my legs.

"Now wait a minute," Sugg said. "We may not do any good, but we're going to try again. It ain't over until the fat lady sings."

We gave the gobbler a few minutes to settle down and then made a wide circle. The area we were hunting was bounded on the west by the creek and on the east by a large pasture. Sugg was afraid the gobbler was going to head out into the pasture before we had a chance to coax him our way. We heard the gobbler sing out again; he was very near the edge of the field. We sat down by another large oak and Sugg pulled out a box call his father had given him several years before his death. Three soft yelps and the gobbler had fallen for Sugg's mimicry again.

The way we were situated, there was a small tree obstructing part of my view.

"You see him?" Sugg whispered.

"No," I answered.

"You see that fox squirrel?"

"No."

"He's in that tree right out in front of us."

"No."

I thought, "Oh great, the turkey is going to be in my lap before I see him." Then, about 50 yards away, the gobbler appeared almost magically. The brightness of the open field projected an aura around the bird as he edged his way into the subdued light of the oak bottom. As he puffed up and strutted a few steps, I could see his beard dragging through the grass.

Suddenly, my lungs seemed about to burst. I was breathing loudly and rapidly, but I couldn't get enough air. My mind was racing, but it latched on to the fact I must be about to hyperventilate. That would be all I needed. First I miss a dead-still turkey at 20 yards and now I'm going to pass out before I even get a shot. I guess I'll have to give up hunting and outdoor writing and join a monastery in the far reaches of Outer Mongolia.

"Exhale, David, exhale," I told myself as I panted like an overweight bird dog on an August afternoon. Sugg suggested I sounded much more like a "grizzly bear."

Meanwhile, Sugg had enticed the bird closer. He would strut a few steps, drop down, and move a little closer. The longbeard seemed oblivious to danger. He was determined to impress that imaginary hen that kept yelping sweet nothings his way.

On our trek into the woods, I asked Sugg what the range of his gun was. "About 45 yards," he answered. I had no intention of testing that if I could help it. When we set up, I had picked out a sapling I estimated to be about 30 yards away. I planned on shooting any gobbler that set foot inside that territory. Although he was on a tacking course, zig-zagging to try to get the hen's attention, the gobbler headed straight for my sapling, where the bead of the shotgun rested, although not too steadily. Luckily, I was not out of position this time. My mind focused on the bead and the fast-approaching turkey. "Do I swing and shoot, or do I wait and hope he walks in front of the barrel?" Then I heard words coming from Sugg.

He was trying to tell me to wait until the bird comes out of his strut to shoot. That way, I'd have more neck to shoot at.

"Wait until he comes out..."

"BOOM!"

The turkey had stepped past the sapling and I could wait no longer. My brain had to have oxygen and my mind had mistakenly interpreted Sugg's coaching as a signal to shoot.

The gobbler went down in a heap, flapping its wings, but going nowhere. Sugg won the footrace to the bird and his boot pinned the turkey's neck to the ground. Sugg knocked me sideways with the first congratulatory backslap. I felt obliged to return the favor. After handshakes, a round of general whooping and hollering followed.

I had finally restored my ego to full strength. And, it turned out to be a top-notch bird with a 10 $\frac{1}{2}$-inch beard and spurs of 1 $\frac{1}{8}$ and 1 $\frac{1}{4}$ inches. We loaded the bird into my game bag and the adrenalin was still pumping when I realized—"We've got to cross 'the cable bridge' again."

"I don't know whether me and this turkey will ever get across the bridge," I said.

"Well, if you don't mind walking a little farther, I think I know where we can cross the creek," Sugg said.

We walked a quarter-mile down the creek until the best-looking birch tree I'd seen in a long time came into view. It had succumbed to the erosion of the creek bank and had fallen straight across the creek. Crossing it was like walking on a sidewalk compared to the bridge.

And the extra half-mile walk back to the car was like a stroll down the block, especially with my bird of redemption strapped to my back.

Shade Steele

SWIFT FLOWS THE RIVER

Mabry Anderson

Mabry Anderson, Clarksdale, is Executive Director of the Mississippi Agricultural Aviation Association and the Outdoor Columnist for Farm Press Publication. *He is a free-lance writer for magazines, and the author of two books—*Outdoor Observation, *and* Low and Slow.

E ven above the moan of the wind through the cottonwoods we could hear the roar of the river below us. Surging yellow water eddied around the bluff bank, sucking at our flimsy little boat that appeared puny in the half-light of dawn. Faintly, ever so faintly, we could make out the outline of our island, a mile or more upriver, and as we stood silently watching the sweep of the water, the spine-chilling call of geese blended with the sounds of the river country.

As the light improved we hastily stowed our gear—guns, decoys, shells, and miscellaneous equipment—taking care that the load would be evenly distributed over the bottom of the boat. Log stumps and driftwood swept by, silent reminders of floodwater to come, and I watched their passage with a feeling akin to awe. Years of hunting along old Father of Waters' twisting, changing course have done nothing to lessen my respect for its might, and as always, we fastened our life-belts with care.

"You know," grunted Potts, "every time I walk down that bluff bank and get a good look at that big, mean, old river I'm tempted to walk right back up again! The **Kate Adams** isn't big enough for this son of a gun when she's on a rising rampage."

Silently I agreed. Dangerous water lay between our landing and the island, but Canada geese make men do funny things. There are easier and safer goose bars than our island, but somehow it suits us best. Completely cut off from the mainland, its thousand acres of yellow sand and its slender mud-bar, infested with coontail grass and switch-willow, attract geese by the hundreds. Frankly, we are selfish with our island, and its very inaccessibility wards off all but a few of our locality's many hunters.

Oddly enough, we usually wait until the season is nearly over before turning our efforts toward geese. Then, after the bar walkers and moon shooters have had their fling, we cruise the river in search of a suitable spot. When the river is low, our island is usually productive. A few days before, we had routed literally hundreds of geese from the mud-bar that comprises its westward side. Without hesitation we had dug our pit in its geographical center and carefully rigged a cover that perfectly matched the terrain. Shooting had been well-nigh perfect, but the winter rise had come, steadily encroaching upon our bar, inching nearer and nearer to our pit.

"Today'll be our last day on the island," announced Potts. "By tomorrow, the pit'll be under two feet of water."

Without replying I pushed the boat away from the bank, and as we hit the channel, Potts jerked the motor to life. The current on a rising river is unbelievably strong, and glances at the shoreline revealed that our progress was almost negligible. Carefully Potts twisted the little boat this way and that, feeling out the currents in an effort to find easier going. Warily I watched the water ahead, alert for drifting logs that can wreck a boat without warning.

Suddenly, with almost startling intensity, a clamor reached our ears that could be heard above the roar of the motor and the river. A glance at the island revealed the cause of the noise—geese by the hundreds were

44

rising from our bar, from around the very rim of our pit, it seemed! Fascinated, we watched as they towered aloft and strung out across the leaden sky, bound for the cornfields that lie between the river and the levee. Their pattern is always the same: they roost on the bars, and at daybreak they stream to the cornfields. For an hour or two they will feed, and then they return to the river, searching for sand, water, and green stuff.

After what seemed an eternity, we passed our pit and docked the boat on the bar a quarter of a mile away. I secured the line to a stake well up on the bar as insurance against being inadvertently marooned. Quickly we unloaded our gear and struck out across the mud-flat, bound for the pit. Ducks and geese were awing, and in every direction we could see them. In long, wavering lines the geese drove toward the cornfields, but the ducks, happy over rising waters that inundated new crops of food, milled aimlessly about. Many passed over within easy range, but we left them alone, intent upon larger game. Suddenly, as we neared the pit, eight Canadas appeared from down-river, low to the water and headed our way.

"Down!" snapped Potts, and without changing our stride, we flattened our bodies against the grass-covered sod.

Stone-still we lay, hoping against hope that the birds would continue on their established line of flight, but such luck was not to be. Almost casually, it seemed, they veered away, disappearing into the haze that rolled up from the west.

Upon reaching the pit I began placing the decoys while Potts cleaned house. A sand ridge runs for the length of the mud-bar, sprinkled lightly with willow shoots and grass. Goose sign was rampant, the mud being a welter of tracks and the willows virtually shredded. Quickly I worked, staggering our rather large set-up to our mutual liking. Twenty-eight birds in all are used, sixteen of them being the conventional three-dimensional folding kind and the remaining twelve tremendous, homemade affairs sawed from plywood. These big boys are the attractors, and have proved their value time without number.

Rapidly I worked, scattering them widely and letting them face in every direction. Some goose hunters frown on this procedure, preferring that each decoy face directly into the wind, but Potts and I prefer our method. We are convinced, from hours of observation, that feeding or resting geese pay scant attention to wind direction, so long as they remain unfrightened. However, the majority of our birds put in their appearance from the south, so we usually place the greater number of our decoys so as to present a full profile toward that direction.

Suddenly I was startled by a muted cry from Potts, and without looking up I dived for the pit. Down, down we crouched, and from far up the river I heard the cause of his cry. Geese were on the wing, apparently headed our way, and a quick peek through the interlocked branches that covered the pit was a revealing sight. At least thirty big Canadas came loafing along, but Potts' words were far from comforting.

"They'll never make it," he breathed. "Don't think they saw us but the decoys are not right. You can't fool that big a drove of geese with half a set-up."

As usual, Potts was right. He's hunted geese for a good many years, and he can usually call the turn. For a moment, it appeared that they might come in; their cries were strident as they spotted the decoys.

But then, without warning, they veered away, swinging past us, high and far out. As we watched, they turned completely and glided to a landing on the sand itself, three-quarters of a mile up the bar!

"Damn!" growled Potts. "There goes the goose hunt unless we move those babies. Every bird that shows up will see 'em, and our decoys can't compete with that sort of competition!"

To make bad matters worse, an intervening bluff of sand lay between our pit and the birds, and to flush them would either mean opening up with our guns or a half-mile walk. For a moment we debated our predicament, deciding against firing our guns. Unnecessary shooting can ruin a hunt quickly, and then again we may need those geese before the day is over. If resting geese can be put to flight without frightening them too much, there is always the possibility of their returning. However, instead of using good judgement and trekking up the bar immediately to put them aloft, I returned to the decoys and finished the set-up.

Returning to the pit, Potts proposed, "Want to toss to see who'll walk up those geese?"

"Nope," I replied. "Let's sit here a while. Maybe birds from the south won't notice 'em."

For a while we sat silently, meditating upon those geese and absorbing the wild beauty of the river country. At our backs, only seventy-five yards away, the rising river gurgled, and at our front the floodwater had crept up a little ravine until we were situated almost on an island on an island. Grass and willows were thick along the water's edge, and the ducks made merry around us. Over our heads they streamed, oblivious to our presence and intent only on their feeding. In huge rafts they lit along the river's edge, only to be swept along by the surging current like miniature ducks at a carnival shooting gallery. Downstream they bobbed, but upon reaching the channel they fluttered upward, only to repeat the performance.

No geese were in evidence, this being the slow period between dawn and the return of the cornfield feeders. Occasional cries from the geese on the sand-bar could be heard, and again Potts suggested that we put them to flight. Somehow I knew that his suggestion was sound, but we were both reluctant to leave the pit. The minutes wore on, and then, almost unexpectedly, we heard the cries of returning birds!

Cautiously we peered through the slits in the pit cover, and directly to our right eight wavering forms could be seen on the horizon. Evidently they were bearing directly down on us, and suddenly, by the increased tempo of their cries, we knew that they had spotted the decoys. On, on they came, lowering steadily until they loomed like giants in the sky.

A few more seconds and they would be within range, but then, without warning, the thing that we feared began. Those blasted geese on the sand-bar screamed their greetings aloft, begging and pleading, and without a moments's hesitation our birds veered away, not twenty-five yards beyond range! Like an arrow to its mark they bored their way up the bar and alighted amid the squalling geese without even a preliminary circle.

Silently Potts flipped a coin and, as usual, I lost. Over the side of the pit I clambered, turning northward and keeping the bluff sand-bank between the geese and me. My strategy was to get well above the birds before putting in my appearance, and the topography of the bar served my purpose admirably. Actually, the sand-bar portion of the island is twenty feet higher than the mud-bar, and as I walked rapidly along, I mentally estimated how far I must walk before arriving at a point well above them. With luck those geese might turn southward and cross the pit, offering a shot to Potts.

Well above my quarry, I peered cautiously over the rim of the sand-bank. Three hundred yards out they stood, snaky heads erect, watching, always watching. I flattened myself against the sand and began my slithering stalk.

Suddenly they towered aloft! The noise of a rising flock is a spine-tingling sound, and I lay there on the sand, awed by its pagan beauty. Up, up they towered, clamoring and shrieking and turning downwind as soon as they were airborne. Straight toward the pit they bored, climbing rapidly and passing directly over Potts' head, much too high. Disgruntled, I retraced my footsteps, relieved at least that our competition had departed.

Again we took up our vigil, content to remain silent and to constantly scan the sky. A glance at my watch revealed that the hour was growing late, and as we watched, three high-flying flocks of returning geese traded by. We started to fidget, turning to the thermos bottle of coffee to break the monotony. The witching hour was almost past, and we began to regret not having bagged a limit of ducks from the many opportunities earlier in the day.

Then, oddly enough, I saw geese on the horizon before hearing their call. A thin line, reminiscent of a spiderweb that appears and disappears from view, was strung lightly across the

Kenner Patton

southern sky. The line grew sharper as we watched; they were geese, that much we could tell, heading our way and quite low to the water. Carefully we pulled grass over the observation slits in the pit cover, more through nervousness than through necessity.

Rapidly the wavering line developed into seventeen geese, but how slowly they travel when heading your way! Their cries by now were constant, and as they drew nearer and nearer we held our collective breaths. Lower and lower they dropped, talking contentedly to the decoys, and my hand tightened automatically on the gunstock. As I watched through a minute opening in the pit top they suddenly set their wings and glided straight toward the pit; but then, almost hesitantly, their wing-beats resumed and they passed overhead, a bit too high.

This is the worst moment that ever comes to a goose hunter. Birds overhead, perhaps at extreme shotgun range, and what shall you do? If you shoot and miss, you'll grumble for days, but if you let them by and they don't return, that's even worse—if possible. Some mental telepathy between us caused us to hold our fire, and when they were safely past us I risked a glance in their direction. They were turning back, talking to the decoys, and I knew intuitively that this time they would come right in. Past us again they streamed, almost within range, and then they turned back upwind and pedaled down, black feet feeling for the bar. Like winged boxcars they loomed before us, and in a flash we were up!

Somehow I missed cleanly with my first attempt. Things happen too fast at a time like this, and I always grow just a little bit panicky. Quickly I turned the gun toward a climbing gander that hung before me like a B-29. This time my aim was better, and at the bark of the gun he staggered, but failed to fall! Those babies are tough, make no mistake about it, and as he slowly continued aloft I desperately let loose with my remaining shell. This time the hold was good, and like a blockbuster bomb he hurtled to the bar, neck flung backward and dead in the air. Potts had killed cleanly with his one and only shot, and with a salute to the departing birds we scrambled from the pit and retrieved our kill.

We had bagged our birds, and already the hunt was over. There are some who decry a bag limit that allows only one bird per day, but as we stood on the bar and admired our take we were quite content. Somehow the fellow that counts his success by the weight of his bag has missed the very essence of hunting. True, we can look backward with a feeling of nostalgia to those lost days when heavy bags were common and permissible, but so long as we are granted the privilege of roaming the river country and drinking in the wild beauty of an untrammeled land I shall not raise my voice in protest against necessarily low bag limits. The game itself is the thing, and I shall remember how that lordly old gander looked as he plummeted earthward long after I have forgotten heavier and easier bags.

"Yep," murmured Potts, as if in answer to my unspoken thoughts, "this is our last day on the island for the season. By tomorrow morning the pit will be gone."

Yes, our season was over, but another winter would come. Again we'd return to the river to listen to the sullen mutter of surging waters, to the sighing of the wind through cottonwoods and willows, and to the call of geese on the wing. The seasons pass all too quickly: spring, summer, autumn, then winter again. Swift flows the river.

EXPERIENCING WONDERS OF HUNTING—A NEW YEAR'S TRADITION

Jim Ewing

Jim Ewing, Canton, is an award-winning editorial writer for The Jackson Clarion-Ledger, *and former editor of* Mississippi Out-of-Doors, *the official newspaper of the Mississippi Wildlife Federation for three years.*

No football bowl games for me today! No sir, I'm out enjoying a tradition that I've carried forth over the years. I've gone duck hunting.

I am simply incredulous when I hear someone make disparaging remarks about hunting. To my mind, it's incredible such ideas aren't challenged. The joys of hunting are just too numerous.

For example, one of the great joys I find is being with my dog, Dixie. At the house, Dixie is just a dog. She barks a lot, scratches a lot, eats a lot, and generally hangs around the house like dogs do.

Out in the swamps duck hunting, though, Dixie is not just a dog.

She scrambles through brambles, crashes through ice, and swims deep water to retrieve what ducks are shot. She is enlivened, becomes a different animal, and we both revel in that normally hidden wildness.

She also is a companion. She's patient, doesn't criticize, and rarely gets in the way. And, after years of hunting together, each knows the other's moods and afflictions. As great as love between humans can be, the relationship between dog and man is a bountiful, enduring mystery, too.

But dogs alone don't make hunting enjoyable. It's more. Too many Americans are too removed from nature. Many must think meat comes in a package from the grocery (parented by plastic bags, no doubt). Many don't take responsibility for what they eat. Responsibility? Think on it.

There is no moral superiority to being anti-hunting, but quite the reverse. Cows are just as Bambi-eyed as any elusive deer and a heckuva lot more cows, like veal calves, lambs, pigs, and fat chickens find their way to America's dinner tables than hunter-killed game.

How is killing a cow or chicken, which has virtually zero chance at escape, more acceptable than a hunter tracking (and usually being outsmarted by) elusive wild game? Because of scarcity? Not on game animals. The licenses, taxes, and fees hunters pay all go to provide for game in its wild state. It's ignoring and losing habitat that wipes out wildlife, not hunting.

Do anti-hunters feel morally superior because they are physically removed from the kill? If so, supermarkets have a greater spiritual significance than I thought. Because there is a farmer, a grocer, and a butcher standing between the consumer and an animal, doesn't the consumer actually pull the trigger to kill a helpless animal every time he plunks down his dollar for meat?

No, even if reincarnated as an animal, I'd choose to be the fox and not the hen, the deer and not the cow. I don't apologize for being a hunter and, in my view, no one should. But neither do I hunt to join in philosophical debates.

When I go into the woods with my gun and dog I'm 100,000 years old. The meat I provide for the table, I provided with my weapon and with

53

my dog. I outsmarted the animal. I killed the animal. I cleaned the animal by removing its fur or feathers and entrails with my own hands. I cooked the animal and I ate it. And it makes me feel good. And I can live and hunt again.

Basic? Yes. Very happily so, as in such other "uncivilized" or unfashionable concepts as: survival, independence, self-reliance, skill....

And there is a sense of awe. When I call to the ducks and they call back, warily circling, gliding, responding, we are dancing to an ancient tune. The hunter and the hunted. The seeker and the sought. The predator and its prey. It is as awesome and as natural as the balance between night and day.

The chase has its rewards, too. The ducks have been late to arrive this year. So, my hunting buddy, Ernest, and I have been forced to range farther afield. Only a few days ago, we tried some oxbow lakes along the Mississippi-Louisiana border. We traveled down bayous, through narrow waterways, called "chutes," and, at times, had to shut down the motor, poling by hand instead.

As we continued along our exploration, however, we saw ahead the dark woods become lighter, the trees falling away. Through the flooded timber we went, until the channel became wide again, and then we gently moved into the stream. And there before us like an ocean suddenly lay the Mississippi River.

Now I know how DeSoto felt when he trekked across Mississippi to confront his Father of Waters. The awe it inspires spans beyond the times of mere humans. And it's a force that binds creatures of fur, feather, and man's naked flesh.

It's difficult to explain the feeling of experiencing nature and participating in the awesome forces that comprise it. Poling through woods in the teeth of bitterly cold winds to witness America's mightiest river firsthand, as opposed to looking down at it from an insulated auto on a man-made bridge, is the difference between merely having life and being truly alive. It's the difference between hunting game and shopping at the grocery.

And maybe it's apt, too, that on New Year's Day I'm out hunting. It's the start of a new year, a new quest with new and elusive goals to pursue, their successful capture, and sights seen along the way unknown.

They call it "hunting," not "finding." And each day is a new quest.

S.W. (Beau) Neill

Kenner Patton

SQUIRREL HUNTING: LET THE DOG WORK

George Warner

George Warner, Meridian, is a Chancery Judge and former District Attorney. An outdoor newspaper columnist, George free-lances also, covering hunting, fishing, mountain climbing, scuba diving, and cooking. He is the author of one book—Get Outdoors 'n Kookin' The Katch.

I jumped straight up when Daddy grabbed my toe. Had been lying there wide awake WITH my eyes closed and dreaming up a storm. You know what I mean. I had been awake all night long while I was sleepin'. That's total excited expectation for an eight-year-old boy.

You see, I was going squirrel hunting! Not still hunting, real hunting. Where the dog does all the work and you have all the fun. The leaves had dropped, and Mac was ready with his dog. It was 4:00 a.m. and time to go. We ate big, and headed for small, small Pace in the Delta.

Mac was the local blacksmith. He and his mutt, Sport, waited at the shop. Few folks today know a "smith" or ever saw a blacksmith's shop. The local "smith" was the most needed man in town. He fixed everything. If you had somethin' broke and Mac could not either fix it or duplicate it in his shop, you didn't need it anyway. When the shops closed, everything started to break down. Today, half the folks I know are in some kind of service or repair business. Anyway—off to the big woods near Gunnison—over the levee—between the levee and the Mississippi River.

My first squirrel hunt! Like a big-game safari. The first time away from the fields near home.

'N the squirrels were everywhere. Old Sport worked like heck. Fast as we shot one, he treed another. That was some dog! Delta's best.

Some say fox and grey squirrels do not band together. That's only so where they live apart. In those woods, we killed both kinds and a few blacks—beautiful and solid black. We even shot some white or albinos through the years. But fox are the biggest—up to three pounds. Greys seldom top a pound.

I don't claim to remember all the details. Too long ago. I can see the first squirrel, though—in a fork barking at Sport. They usually hid, but not this one—and solid black! My little 410 put him in the sack.

• I remember when they got real high in the tall hardwoods. I just stung 'em, then Mac's ole double hammer 12 helped 'em down.

• I remember seeing Lost Lake where Mac and a friend killed 26 mallards with three shots from two double 12's. Let's save that story for later.

• I remember and cherish my friendship and learning experiences with Mac through my growin' up years.

• I remember he always hugged Little George after each trip and I hugged him back and thanked him. And I don't remember ever noticing the difference in the color of our skin.

• I remember I was hooked on squirrel hunting with a dog. More than 40 years later I got me a dog—a real champion. He may not be as good as Calico, the super champion of Wadell Robinson, but my dog is good—darned good. He had already been named the name he has now—Sport. Every time I call him it takes me back to that first hunt and those years with Mac and his Sport. Yep, you can mouth memories. Squirrel hunting with a dog is completely different from still hunting in October and November. Here's a few tips I have learned. There are lots more some of you know, so pass 'em on to me.

1. The easiest way to find where squirrels live is to find hardwoods with nests. Even if den trees are present, squirrels build nests. Generally there is about one squirrel per nest in the area.

2. Make all the noise you want to. Take the family. This is a relaxed family sport and a walk through the woods. The dog does the hunting. You do the walkin', carryin', and the hard part—the searching the trees. Let the dog hunt-and-tree and then call you. Just enjoy the woods.

3. Take a 12 gauge for the tall trees and a .22 for clumps and nests. Sometimes you have to bust a few clumps to make old bushy-tail jump. I have seldom gotten one out of nests, don't really know why. Usually they are in the vines and forks. Caution: Shoot as little as possible. A lot of shots and no squirrels and you will ruin a good dog.

4. Do not shoot if the dog has not treed (unless you see a squirrel). The dog will become confused. He wants to show you—it's his show—it's his job. Let him do it. If you keep shooting or pulling vines he will quit and wait for you to find squirrels for him.

5. When the dog trees, think like a squirrel. Where would you hide if a dog ran you up the tree he is barkin' at? That's usually where old bushy-tail is. A fork, a clump of leaves, a mess of vines, etc. Not necessarily in the same tree. Usually in a tree with vines, and seldom in a nearby nest.

6. Is there a good cover tree in travelin' distance? That's probably where he is. He went up where the dog treed and travelled next door to hide. If there are pines around, pity you! Move to another area. You cannot find squirrels in pines and there are usually no vines to shake. If a pine is nearby with vines, give it a good shake. Good odds that is where you get supper.

7. Shake the vines in all the nearby trees. One person shakes, all others watch. Bushy will move and you must see him. When you shoot a squirrel, be sure and let the dog "mouth" him.

8. Do not point to nests and have the dog bark. He will quit hunting and let you tree for him. Remember, it is fun for you but it's serious business to a good dog. You can ruin him if you don't watch out.

9. Be sure and pat your dog and thank him after he mouths the squirrel. If you cannot find ole Bushy, still thank your dog and pat him. It's your fault, not his.

10. Believe your dog. The squirrels are there. If you are finding less than half he trees, look closer and shake more vines. But don't blame the dog. The squirrels are holding much closer now than when I was a boy. They used to sit and bark at the dog. Now they are the very devil to rout out.

11. If your dog ranges too far, finds few squirrels, won't bark or tree, and won't chase cripples, sell him or give him away. A good squirrel dog is the greatest. A cruddy one is an experience in exasperation to be avoided.

12. Lastly, a good dog will do things you wouldn't believe. Sport treed for me and mouthed the squirrel I shot. He still barked and refused to leave. I shook a few more vines and out came two more squirrels!

I remember one day Mac's Sport showed his stuff. A large fox squirrel jumped to a tree across a creek. Mac shot him on the other side. Sport hit the icy water, got the squirrel, and swam back with him. Labs do it all the time with ducks, but a squirrel dog? My Sport hasn't pulled that trick out of his bag yet.

Shortly after my first hunt, I had to write a poem for English class. Here is that poem:

We arose at four and started,
Eating breakfast at my home.
Then on to Concordia Woods,
Where the squirrels feed and roam.
When we first saw daylight,
We were passing Waxsaw Station.
Soon we joined other hunters,
At the Sunnywild Plantation.
When the sun came out to greet us,
We had a squirrel up a tree.
As I was just a tenderfoot,
They gave the first squirrel to me.
Bang! went my Winchester,
Down the squirrel came.
To the others it looked so small,
To me it was big game.
The day was filled with pleasure,
Ole Sport hunted until late.
Tho I was just a tenderfoot,
During the day I killed eight.
That night when we ate supper,
I was too exhausted to move about.
But I would have burst my belly,
If my jawbones had held out.

I guess that poem strikes many as very juvenile. Sure—I agree. But looking back and reading it through the eyes of an eight-year-old, it's quite right.

You see, to an eight- or ten-year-old, a squirrel hunt with a dog is the greatest. I'm much older now and it still is the greatest. Plan yourself a trip to the Super Bowl, a cruise on the Carla "C", and a weekend at the theater in New York. All three combined will not produce the excitement for your son or daughter as a good squirrel hunt with a champion dog.

Remember, the thing the kids like most of all is being with you. Have you got a youngster, boy or girl? Mention to them a woods romp with a dog. See their eyes? Now you know. See that smile on their faces? Well, go for it. That's what parents are for. That's what "familyin'" is all about.

What's that? You don't have a dog? Well, give me a call. Me 'n Sport would love to go.

Get Outdoors!

EVERY BOY SHOULD HAVE A DRUM

Jim Martin

Jim Martin, Biloxi, is a syndicated newspaper columnist and free-lance writer for both television and magazines. He is the Eastern Gulf Editor for Saltwater Sportsman Magazine *and Mississippi Editor for* Gulf Coast Fisherman Magazine.

S pray from the bow of the 15-footer was cold enough to sting, although the late December day had been relatively mild. I hunkered down a little lower now as I steered for the slender creosote piling marking the northeastern corner of the low-profile reef we planned to fish. From the center seat, anticipation and excitement fairly glowed from the face of my nine-year-old son, Bill, as he clenched his favorite pole with whitened knuckles.

The trip had been planned, cancelled, re-scheduled, and cancelled again for various reasons, but at last we were about to sample some honest-to-goodness winter fishing on Mississippi's Gulf Coast.

I cut the motor about 75 yards from the marker and gently eased the anchor over the side into 10 feet of water. In no time at all, the slack went out and the light-weight fiberglass skiff snapped smartly around into the northeast wind.

Bill and I looked at one another in the strange silence, then together watched the spectacle of a beautiful winter sunset. There was only one other boat on the reef, and as we watched, one of the anglers suddenly stood up, locked his reel, and struck back hard. We were really interested now as the lucky fisherman's rod bowed sharply as the hooked fish began a long, powerful run.

"What do you think he has, Daddy, a redfish?"

"Could be a big red," I answered, "or maybe a black drum. Water's a bit cold for sharks this late in the season.... If this light holds for a few more minutes we may see what he has."

But the light didn't last as the man seemed to battle the fish interminably. Finally, as we strained to pierce the gathering darkness, we heard the man swear lustily as he lost the big fish at boatside. Much to our surprise, they soon pulled up their anchor and left.

"That's odd," Bill mused, "They've just lost a really big fish and going in.... And here we are just starting to fish!"

I leaned back and smiled contentedly. Bill may or may not grow up to become a Rhodes Scholar, but he's going to be one heck of a fine fisherman. Already he was a joy to be with and a quick study.

While Bill was intently watching the man fight his fish, I had been busily cutting up bait and rigging tackle. The trip was planned primarily to catch big fish—reds and drum— but also to lay in a supply of "eating fish" such as sea trout and whiting if they happened to be around. To date, Bill hadn't caught anything larger than a four-pound sheepshead. Hopefully, his luck on bigger fish would change tonight.

I baited two heavy outfits with chunks of fresh mullet, tossed them out, and placed them in rod holders, leaving the reels out of gear but with ratchets left on. Bill and I then baited the two remaining light outfits with medium-sized dead shrimp and pitched them out.

It was full dark now and we could easily see the heavy traffic moving along U.S. Highway 90 a mile to the north of us. Bill was just zipping up his jacket against the increasing chill when the ratchet on one of the big outfits suddenly sounded off. This bite proved a false alarm, however, and was probably caused by a catfish or crab bumping the cut mullet. Even in the darkness I could tell Bill was trembling from the heart-stopping suddenness of the reel going off. I'd be lying if I didn't say it made me jump also; night fishing can do that to you—and after 15 years, it's still exciting.

With nothing much going on, we took advantage of the time to explore the "night lunch" that had been packed for us. In the sack were meat sandwiches, hard cheese, cookies, and a few peppermint candies that were supposed to go in the Christmas stocking a few days hence; well, I said Bill was a quick study!

We made short work of the sandwiches, washing them down with coke, half expecting one or more reels to sound off while our hands were full, but so far the night had been monotonously dull. I figured conditions to be near-perfect, with light winds, clear weather, and a rising tide due to peak at 11:00 p.m. So where were the fish?

After 30 minutes without action, we pulled anchor and moved 100 yards south. This was a big reef, covering several acres at least, and the fish—if indeed there were any—could be anywhere on it. One of the many reasons I enjoy night fishing is the beauty and solitude it affords. Rocking gently in a familiar boat with your number-one fishing buddy with you and a million twinkling stars overhead is a great way to build memories. Ten years from now—looking back—these will have been the good old days—not the days of your youth, of course, but *his*.

Our first action came soon after we had put fresh strips of mullet on the big rigs. The ratchets on both reels went off simultaneously. Bill grabbed one, I the other. My fish was hooked solidly but sure wasn't a heavyweight; after a couple of minutes of hard reeling I had a pound-and-a-half sea trout flopping on the deck. Out of the corner of my eye, I saw that Bill had missed his strike and was hurriedly reeling in to rebait.

"If the small stuff is moving in," I suggested, "let's use the baitcasting rods. It will be more fun and we'll catch more fish."

But Bill was way ahead of me. His shrimp had barely enough time to find bottom when I heard his "grunt and got'cha" that was to begin sounding like a broken record as the evening progressed. Instead of fishing, I chose to keep a spare outfit baited for him. Each time he'd swing a fish aboard, I'd hand him an already-baited rod, kinda like passing a frontiersman a loaded rifle when the Indians were circling the wagons— only these "Indians" were wearing fins instead of feathers! He was doing a fine job on those trout and whiting and the live well amidship was fast becoming crowded.

We had all but forgotten the mullet-baited rods when one of the clickers started making music. Bill quickly put his rod down and snatched the big outfit from its holder. Even in the panic of excitement, I was happy to see he remembered the advice I had given him on what procedures to follow.

He pushed the clicker off first, then the beam of his little flashlight zeroed in on the spool of his reel, revealing line being pulled off at a steady pace. After a few moments, it slowed, stopped, then started again, this time faster.

"*Now*, Daddy?"

"*Now!*" I yelled, and Bill locked the reel and leaned back on him, exerting all the pressure his lean little body could muster. He was rewarded with a jolting surge that propelled him two halting steps forward. Instinctively, I grabbed his belt to keep him from going over the side. This was no pantywaist trout or whiting; he had hooked into the biggest fish of his young life!

We had practiced this drill many times in the backyard, and the training had finally paid off. One thing we hadn't worked out, however, was the *size of the fish*. Suppose Bill couldn't hold on to the runaway freight train—then what?

I needn't have worried. Three minutes into the battle, Bill announced—through gritted teeth—that this was *his* fish, and by golly, he'd land him or lose him on his own.

As it turned out I couldn't have helped him anyway. Five minutes into the struggle, the clicker on *my* reel sounded off and a few seconds later I had my hands full with my own big fish!

Mine was the smaller of the two, and after a few minutes of hard pumping and reeling, I managed to work him to within 20 feet of the boat. Bill yelled that his fish was at last ready for the net, so I "tethered" mine by sticking the rod in the holder and loosening the drag. Did I say things had been dull!?

After some hectic moments we were able to land both fish, which turned out to be black drum rather than the channel bass or "redfish" we were hoping for. But Bill couldn't have been happier. His fish scaled 22 pounds, mine 16. Thirty minutes later, he hooked into an 18-pounder on his little trout rod and fought the fish for almost a half hour before I was able to slip the net under him. I honestly didn't know who was worn out the most—Bill or the fish. After the third big fish came aboard we decided to call it a night. Those drum plus the 30-odd trout and whiting made for a rather fantastic outing for a nine-year-old—for his old dad, too!

We made another trip to that reef about a week later, this time taking Bill's best friend, Ben Belham, along. Two drum were caught, a 20- and a 12-pounder, and Ben got them both. Now, this made quite an impression on the little guy, since his biggest fish prior to this had been a bluegill!

Action on the second trip came late, saving me from a possible nervous breakdown. Trying to keep two active nine-year-olds entertained, from falling overboard, and reasonably still, took more doing than I had imagined. When the drum finally showed, I could almost have kissed them.

After the 20-pounder was safely netted, an amazing change came over the boys. Gone was all the silliness, the jumping around, the endless prattle. They saw what they had accomplished, for the proof lay shimmering at their feet. They were excited, sure, but with a difference... because now they had become *fishermen*. Did I believe every boy should have a drum? Most assuredly!

In my opinion, black drum are the ideal first big fish for kids to cut their piscatorial teeth on. Perhaps not as strong as a lean channel bass, they still have plenty of muscle and are far less dangerous to contend with than, say, a shark or ray.

Black drum are also fairly plentiful, inhabiting both the Atlantic Ocean and Gulf of Mexico. And while they tend to run to a larger size in the Atlantic, as do their close cousin, the channel bass, I firmly believe there are more of them in the Gulf.

On Mississippi's Gulf Coast, there are two distinct "runs" of these fish. The best one, according to veteran pier anglers and jetty jockeys, occurs in February in most years but can begin before or after by as much as two weeks. A lesser run of fish comes along in mid-April but receives less attention because by then other species—notably mackerel and ling—are arriving. A few fish are taken year-round in brackish bays and lakes.

Drum, of course, are by no means a glamour species. Channel bass are handsomer—and stronger, jack crevalle have far more endurance, king mackerel are probably four times faster, and hard-fighting cobia are infinitely better eating.

I suppose the one trait that endears ole *Pogonias cromis* to men and boys—especially boys—is his availability. Here is a fish that can be caught from a pier or jetty in the dead of winter or early spring when nothing else—and I mean *nothing else*—is moving. Very obliging indeed.

In addition to numerous places where land-based anglers can try for a heavy-weight drum—they run up to 60 pounds—there are also some newly constructed inshore oyster shell reefs. The one my son and I fished most often is located a mile from the mainland just a short run westward from the Long Beach Small Craft Harbor. Another fine low profile reef is the White House Reef, also a mile from the mainland and positioned just west of the main entrance to Keesler Air Force Base near Biloxi. Both of these fish producers are well marked by pilings.

While Bill and I enjoy night fishing best, black drum can easily be taken during daylight hours. On this coast, at least, anglers seem to prefer late afternoon fishing, especially when combined with a rising tide. Crab is the preferred bait, and, surprisingly perhaps, best action may come during periods of stormy weather.

I wanted Bill to catch a big channel bass in the worst way last fall but it just wasn't to be. He did manage to hook a couple but wasn't able to drive the hook home solidly enough to hold. The obliging black drum provided a natural solution for him to gain valuable confidence and experience on big fish.

This year he's already talking about trying for a shark, king mackerel, or jack crevalle—any one of which is more than capable of jerking him overboard!

I admire his courage and enthusiasm (a father's right!). The lad has soaked up a lot of salt water savvy in the last couple of years and is ready to graduate to bigger and better things. Come to think about it, an ocean's not a bad classroom.

But I must also salute the lowly black drum—the "ugly duckling" of gamefish—who, just by being himself, helped with the transformation. Do I like drum? Well, let's put it this way—I think every boy should have one.

ARTISTS AND PHOTOGRAPHERS

Sam Beibers, Clinton. Commercial Artist: Beibers Creative Arts.
Jacket design and color art
Paul T. Brown, Brandon. Contractor and Free-lance Photographer.
Color photograph
Lisa Brunetti, Sartaria. Art Teacher and Book Illustrator.
Color art, black and white: pages 126, 143, and 149
Frances Drake, Vicksburg. Art Teacher and Book Illustrator.
Color art and black and white: page 170
Jerrie Glasper, Greenville. Wildlife and Commissioned Artist.
Color art courtesy of the Bill Mayton Collection.
Stephen Kirkpatrick, Jackson. Professional Photographer and Author; His
Marvelous Works Studio.
Color photograph
S.W. (Beau) Neill, Leland. Farmer and Book Illustrator.
Black and white: pages 55, 92, and 100.
Kenner Patton, Leland. Commercial Artist, *Southern Living* Magazine
Black and white: pages 49, 56, and 174
Perry Ritchie, Canton. Commissioned Artist.
Color art
John Allen Smith, Meadville. Professional Photographer; Homochitto Outdoors.
Color photographs
Shade Steele, Alligator. Wildlife Artist; Backwater Studios.
Color art and black and white: pages 15, 28, 42, 196 and 198
Glenn Warren, Jackson. Commissioned Artist.
Color art

John Allen Smith

Shade Steele

Lisa Brunetti

Frances Drake

Paul T. Brown

Stephen Kirkpatrick

Stephen Kirkpatrick

Jerrie Glasper

THE CANINE TRACKER

Paul T. Brown

Paul Brown, Brandon, is a specialty building contractor. Paul is also a free-lance writer and photographer for various magazines.

Mention a special hunting dog during deer season and most hunters immediately think of a beagle, a walker, a black and tan, or some other special breed of running dog. Scenes of howling hounds chasing a big buck dominate their thoughts.

There are, however, other special dogs being used in conjunction with deer hunting in Mississippi. Their purpose is not that of pushing deer to a hunter, but rather to find wounded deer, those that cannot be found otherwise.

These trail dogs, often called trackers or blood trailers, can make a hunter mighty happy when he recovers a trophy that could not be found by any other means. Hunters have been known to get down on their knees and kiss the dog square on the mouth. That is the only part of the assignment the dog hates.

If every shot taken on a deer were a killing shot, there would be no need for a trailing canine. Unfortunately, not every shot puts the animal down immediately. Whether hunting with a bow, muzzleloader, shotgun, or rifle, there is always a possiblility that a well-intended shot will turn into some serious trailing. Far too often the animal dies and the hunter never finds his trophy.

But it does not have to end this way. There are well-trained dogs scattered across the state that are making quite a name for themselves. They are finding the deer that man cannot find on his own.

Sam Munro, a retired Jackson fireman, has such a dog. Max, a black Labrador retriever, has found 184 deer over his eight years of tracking wounded deer.

Many of the hunters are after their first deer. Many are kids, and others are just giving deer hunting a first try. Therefore, many of the shots are not the kind that drop a buck in his tracks.

"Very seldom do people know when they hit a deer that it is gutshot," Sam says. "And the gut-shot deer is the hardest to find. It goes further and leaves the least amount of evidence. You can't even notice the moisture drippings, but the dog knows it."

Sam feels that a good trail dog is a must in his situation and vital to most deer hunters. "Nobody wants to see an animal suffer," Sam says. "And nobody wants to lose one once he has shot it. I have hunted all my life and dreamed of owning a blood-trailing dog. I lost numerous deer, especially bowhunting. I had friends lose deer. I decided to do something about it.

"I am by a long shot no dog expert. It was just a lucky stroke that I happened to do this and it worked.

"You take a running dog and try it with them and the next thing you know they're off running a deer or rabbit. I had always been a duck hunter and when I quit duck hunting, I gave my good duck dog away. After that I just always yearned to have another Lab. So I got another one. And there I was still dreaming of having a blood-trailing dog; so the first deer I killed that year, I took the feet and some blood and trained Max."

Sam claims anybody can train a Lab to blood trail. His method is so simple. It seems too easy. He explains, "What I did to train Max was to take one of the feet and dip it into some deer blood and make a trail. I left the foot at the end of the trail and went back and got Max. I walked him to near the beginning of the trail. He immediately followed the trail and found the foot. That's it! He was trained. He's been finding deer since then. The first deer I put him on was during muzzleloader season. He found him and has not stopped since."

Certainly, this is a simple training procedure, at least on the surface. But a good foundation must be laid in order to train a dog as Sam has done.

A loving relationship between man and dog must be established. "The rapport you build with a dog to make him want to please you is the No. 1 thing it is going to take to train one," Sam says. "You've got to show them a lot of love, play with them, and spend a lot of time with them.

"If I had it to do over, I would teach Max to bark when he finds a deer. I think you can do this by giving him a piece of meat when he finds the foot and making him speak.

"Far too often when you are trailing at night, the dog is going to lose you, so he needs to bark when he finds his 'foot' (the deer), wanting that piece of meat. You can then cut a small piece from the deer for his reward."

Just like many hunters, Max lives for deer season. He really loves his method of hunting. He wants to please Sam. And he usually does. In truth, Max astounds Sam.

"Last year this guy came to the house and said that he had heard I had a dog that could blood-trail deer," Sam recalls. "He had hit the first deer he had ever shot at with a bow. He shot it right at dusk and had followed it until about 10 o'clock that night. He never found his arrow and never found any blood on anything. Well, he went back the next morning and looked until 10 o'clock that morning. He still found nothing. So then he came and got me."

Sam told the man he should have come the night he shot the deer. Even Sam thought it would be hard for Max to find the deer after so many hours had passed.

"We went down there and took the dog in the direction he said the deer went," Sam continues. "Nothing. He said, 'Well, maybe it went in this direction.' We went that way and each time we went a long ways into the woods.

"When we came back to where we started, I said, 'I'm going around this way back to the truck.' He said, 'Well, I know that's the only way the deer did not go.'

"We didn't walk 50 yards and Max started smelling one spot real hard. I went over to him and sure enough there was one drop of dried blood. We started following Max. He went in a straight line to a big creek. When he got to the creek he took a right and followed the creek until it ran into another smaller creek. Well, Max just jumped in the creek, swam to the other side and went about 50 yards, and all of a sudden he hung a left and swam across the big creek. The man that shot the deer was having a tough time keeping up with the dog. But just after we crossed the creek, there was the dead deer.

"Now that was 17 hours after the deer was shot. It was 500 yards and across the two creeks. We never saw any blood after that first drop."

Max has performed feats such as this many times. Sam has witnessed numerous trailing episodes. Some have been baffling, some astonishing and some even down-right humorous.

Sam's stepson, Mark, shot a deer one evening and could not find it. "We took the dog over there and he picked up the trail and ran a pretty good ways," Sam remembers. "Then we heard the dog bay. I knew where he was—in a lake. When I pulled up and shined the spotlight in the water, there was the deer, dog, and an alligator in about the same space as a pickup truck."

Sam naturally has developed confidence in his dog. Yet with all of the deer Max has found, Sam must remind himself that Max knows what he is doing. Just as a woodsman has to learn to trust his compass, a hunter with a trail dog must learn to put faith in his bloodhound.

"Once you have taken the dog out there, you already have admitted that you don't know where the deer is, so don't argue with the dog," Sam says as if talking to himself as much as anyone. "Every time I have argued with Max, he has made a fool out of me. Here I am the one saying don't argue with him and I say, 'No, the deer went over here,' but he'll go over there and that will always be the way the deer went.

"When you are hunting from a tree, fire a shot and then get down, you are in a different world and don't realize it. Things look different. It is hard to tell exactly which direction the deer went after the shot."

Max's dependability rivals the accuracy of a compass. Sam can count on Max going in the right direction. It is up to Sam to keep pace as Max follows his nose.

Max is nearly nine years old now. Sam is not sure if Max can continue his exploits. So Sam is preparing for Max's retirement. Waiting in the wings is a beautiful chocolate Lab named Fudge. The young Lab is batting 1.000 as he went three for three last season, tracking down all the deer he was set out to find. He will get more work this season.

The concept of using blood-trailing dogs is an idea whose time has come. Most deer that are shot, by whatever means, are going to die sooner or later. The trail dog can put the game into the hands of the hunter rather than a pack of coyotes.

Recovering the deer, once shot, is a very important element in a hunt. It can be heartbreaking to lose a nice buck. I know from experience. That's why I am now training a nine-month-old Lab. I hope I never have to put her on a blood trail. But if I continue to hunt, I am sure I will. If not one I shoot, then one shot by a hunting partner or one of my kids. Only this time, I will be prepared.

As Sam says, "The use of blood-trailing dogs is one of the grandest things that has happened to deer hunting. If you just put what little time and effort it takes into training one, you'll be rewarded over and over again."

POSTED

S.W. (Beau) Neill

BADGE OF COURAGE

Dan Bowling

Dan Bowling of Brookhaven is department editor for Gulf Coast Fisherman *magazine. He also freelances for* Salt Water Sportsman *magazine and other publications, sometimes under the Alex Seymour byline. He is Industrial Relations Director for the Mississippi Manufacturers Association.*

It's a beautiful day. I should be outside doing something. Even yard work.

Being out in the cool air and warm sunshine would beat sitting inside writing. But, sit I must, because I was in the wrong place at the wrong time.

The wrong place was across the street from two dogs chasing each other around in circles. The wrong time was when the dogs' circle collided with a passing van. The big dog was hurt and snapping at the air in its pain and confusion. I have more sense than to try to help an injured animal so soon after an injury, but the uninjured dog didn't. The playmate ran up to see what was wrong and was about to get eaten alive. So I intervened.

While shooing the unhurt dog away from the snapping jaws, those same jaws locked on my left ankle in a death grip.

After a trip to the emergency room, five stitches, a tetanus shot plus a few smart remarks from the doctor, I'm inside on this beautiful day with an infected ankle and no place to go.

I can walk all right, once I get going, but I have a noticeable limp. Limping down 5th Avenue or even Canal Street in New Orleans would be okay. Limping anywhere in this small town where I know half the people is not okay. Everybody wants to know what happened.

Outdoorsmen can wear certain injuries like a badge of courage. A freshly bandaged hand can be explained with pride. "It's just a scratch. A 40-pound king mackerel laid it open." "Wow," says the questioner, "that must have hurt." "Nah," the fisherman lies, "disinfected it with Budweiser, sewed it up with 20# mono fishing line and caught three more kings—had a great trip." I'd get a haircut when I didn't need one just to tell a story like that in the barber shop.

Then there's the guy with the bad burn across the inside of his wrist. It looks like a red line drawn diagonally from one side to the other. It hurts like fire, but it's worth it to tell how that wahoo ripped off line so fast the reel smoked and your wrist was almost severed before you could move it. A little stupid to have the line across your wrist when a big fish hits and smokes off line, but, it's a great story.

Limping through Wal-Mart and answering the inevitable questions about my limp would be great......if I'd sprained the ankle chasing a mountain goat in the Rockies. Admitting to a dog bite? No thanks. I'll stay right here and write about it. I don't have to look the reader in the eye when I admit that it wasn't a pit bull, doberman or anything fierce that got me. It was a cocker spaniel! Why couldn't a sea lion have nipped my heel when I was salmon fishing in Alaska? Or, even a bluefish while fishing off the mouth of the Mississippi River? Anything but a cocker spaniel in the neighborhood!

The more the embarrassing wound ached the more I envied my scarred buddy from Prentiss. The hair-thin white lines of horizontal scars on either cheek and just above either eye were silent, but eloquent testimony to his turkey calling prowess. Those beautiful scars were badges

94

of courage permanently etched by the claws of a hungry bob-cat who pounced on his head from the rear as he was calling a big gobbler into range to his front.

What a story he had to tell! And the lucky stiff was scarred in the face for the whole world to see and ask how he got those unusual scars. Some guys have all the luck.

I even envied my former neighbor in Pascagoula who sported the imprint of a 7-horsepower Evinrude propeller on his kisser. By omitting a few facts and inventing a few more, he easily changed those scars of stupidity into badges of heroism.

Thank heavens the dog didn't bite me in the face. At least I can hide the injury under a pair of socks.

Now I know how the soldier felt when he got his purple heart injury opening a can of beans in the war zone. At least he was in hostile territory when his hand slipped. Not me, I was just around the corner when the cocker bit.

Well, I've bared my soul to you about my injury. I interrupted this confession to accompany my wife to the supermarket.

At the market, she went one way and I limped off down another aisle to pick up a few items. We got in and out of the grocery store very fast and I saw only two people I knew. About half way home from the store my wife said, "I saw Carol in the store."

"Yes, I saw her, too," I answered. We rode in silence until we were almost home. Then she said, "Carol was horrified to hear that you were bitten on the ankle by a shark!" I drove on in silence.

THE EAST SIDE COVEY

Robert Hitt Neill

Robert Hitt Neill, Leland, is a syndicated newspaper columnist, free-lance writer, and professional storyteller, averaging over 100 appearances per year. He is a publisher and award-winning author of five books: The Flaming Turkey, How to Lose Your Farm in Ten Easy Lessons and Cope With It, Going Home, The Jakes!, *and* The Voice of Jupiter Pluvius.

I t was almost the last day of bird season. February had been warm and wet, far from ideal hunting conditions. I was therefore surprised when my regular shooting companion pulled into the driveway, especially when I saw he had both of his dogs.

I cut off the lawn mower; that's how unseasonably warm it was—I was mowing down the early growth of burr clover, and it was still February! "What's the deal?" I called, wiping the sweat from my brow as I walked over.

"Thought we might give it one last try," he grinned. "D'ya think we could find that East Side Covey without too much trouble?"

"Lotta green stuff; mighty warm," I shook my head. "I doubt the dogs will be able to smell anything." Actually, I had been planning to finish the yard and maybe go fishing.

My buddy was having none of that. "C'mon, Mate," he beckoned, "for old times sake."

I waved toward the lawn mower and headed for the house to get my gun and shells. I didn't even bother to change my sneakers for boots.

The older dog hung his head over the back of the seat and licked my hand in greeting as I slid into the Jeep wagon. At thirteen, he had only hunted with us once since Thanksgiving, and I was glad to see him. "Hey, Old Fella; good to see you up and around." The younger dog rudely crowded his daddy aside to greet me also as we pulled out of the driveway.

The East Side Covey was one of our most dependable coveys. It was located in a twenty-acre pasture next to the woods, only a couple of miles from the house. We had used this covey as a "starter" on many hunts over the years, simply to convince the dogs, especially the young one, that we were out on a business trip. We never shot the singles, because they always flew into the woods. If fewer than a half-dozen got up on the covey rise, we didn't shoot at all, careful to leave seed birds for the next year. Toward the end of each season, like now, the East Side Covey was down to minimum size. I pointed this out to my companion.

"All I want is one bird out of it today," he said as he slowed the vehicle and pulled to the side of the road by the pasture fence. For some reason, he didn't seem to be his usual jolly self. I found out why when he dropped the tailgate. While the young setter bounded enthusiastically out, his father shuffled stiffly to the back and waited until their master picked him up and gently set him down on the gravel. I raised my eyebrows in question.

My friend sighed and gestured toward the old Llewellyn who had accompanied us for so many years. He lowered his voice as if the dog could hear and understand. "The vet says he's on his last legs. Just in case he doesn't make it until next bird season, I thought we'd try to get in one last short hunt." He paused. "I thought he'd like that; d'you think that's wrong?"

Well, I didn't. I have often thought that when my time comes, I would rather check out from a turkey blind, or a deer stand, or a campfire in the woods surrounded by family and friends and laughter and warm memories of hunts shared. This is not meant to be a morbid discussion; all of us will one day go to meet our Maker. If my memory serves, only Enoch and Elijah are recorded as having escaped the Grim Reaper. And we have all had our favorite bird dogs, hounds, and retrievers whom we have loved and lost. My friend's eyes were moist, and I crossed my fingers in hopes that the East Side Covey would cooperate today.

The young son headed at high speed to circle the pasture; it was triangular in shape, bordered by the woods, a treeline, and the roadside fence where we stood. A brier-grown ditch bisected the field from treeline to woods. The old setter moved stiffly across the middle of the field as we loaded our guns and followed.

It was obvious that the aging back legs could no longer traverse quail country. My hunting buddy had to lift his dog over several clumps of johnson grass or sedge grass. Each time the Llewellyn would again surge forward in his arthritic shuffling trot. As we neared the ditch, approaching a spot where a small cane patch blocked our vision of the other side, I swung out to the right and glimpsed a stolid form of speckled white: the youngster, pointed, across the ditch.

"Hey," I called softly, "we've got a...."

My companion shushed me with a warning finger, nodding at the older dog. As the scent of the East Side Covey reached his nostrils, the setter seemingly shed five years. His drooping tail stiffened; his arthritic hindquarters began to raise as his head and shoulders lowered. He crept forward several steps and froze on point—how many times had we seen him like this? Poised and proud in the performance of his sole mission in life, the Llewellyn showed his hunters that the East Side Covey was in residence in that cane patch, unaware that his son was also pointing the birds from the opposite side of the ditch.

We drank in the scene, me deferring to my companion to decide when to flush. Finally, he inhaled deeply and stepped forward, gun at the ready, "Back me up. Let's get just one more bird for the old boy," he muttered.

They could have flushed and wheeled back behind me; they could have been scattered; they could have run, as they sometimes did, down the ditch toward the woods; they could have stayed low to the ground so that we could not have shot because of the pointing younger dog. But the East Side Covey did none of these; the quail flushed from the cane almost straight up, one cockbird seeming to pause lazily twenty feet above the ditch. At the shot, this quail crumpled in a puff of feathers, falling on the old setter's side of the ditch. I had not shouldered my gun, and now I called the young dog off the retrieve.

The elder Llewellyn moved stiffly to the bobwhite and picked it up tenderly. His master knelt to take the bird, then continued kneeling as he hugged his old dog. I averted my eyes.

We walked back to the Jeep with me carrying two guns, and my friend carrying the old setter while the younger one trailed at heel. The East Side Covey whistled, scattered in the edge of the woods.

A month later, the inevitable came to pass, and the veternarian put the aging bird dog to sleep for the last time.

The next Opening Day, we took the young dog—now the older dog—and a ten-month-old Llewllyn puppy to the pasture. The East Side Covey was once again at the cane, fully two dozen strong. Half ran down the ditch and flushed out of range; seven dodged back over our heads; one stayed low in the ditch and made the treeline unscathed; three fanned out close to the ground, escaping to the woods; and one flew almost straight up. My companion dropped it on his first shot while I missed twice on the one headed for the treeline. At my friend's yell, I collared the experienced setter, while the pup made his first retrieve. The cockbird was delivered to my friend's hand proudly, as had been the last quail we had handled from the East Side Covey, taken from this pup's grandfather.

It's good to have dependable friends.

S.W. (Beau) Neill

DEATH OF A KING

Al Strickland

Al Strickland, Natchez, retired as staff writer and Outdoors Columnist for the Natchez Democrat. *He has been succeeded in that capacity by his son, Ronnie—a Strickland has written the Outdoor Column in Natchez for over 35 years.*

"**B**est you give that girth another tug, boy," commented Ed as we saddled our horses. "Can't ever tell if'n Old Granddad will take too kindly to a picture-taking session." Edward L. (Jughead) Jones, our host for the day, was referring of course to the camera that swung from my shoulder.

"That's right, old Buddy," piped Jim Bourgeois, a field man for one of the nation's leading arms companies. "We'll even get the old rooter to say 'cheese' for you if you want him to."

Both were joking with me, of course, but I felt it was only in an effort to hide their true feelings.

Hunting wild boar is nothing to joke about, at least not in Bourgere Swamp. The 750,000-acre game haven, located some 20 miles downriver from historic Natchez on the Louisiana side, affords the twin-state sportsmen a long measure of productive hunting. Its marshy sanctuary embraces white-tailed deer, wild hog, bear, wild turkey, and the usual smaller game. It's also a sure-fire stopover for the thousands of migrating mallards, black duck, geese, and other waterfowl on their long trek down the Mississippi Flyway.

In more recent years it has also become literally infested with nutria and armadillo, and both play havoc with the dogs. At times, they get rather stubborn in their desire to give chase, and seem to nurse a very special dislike for the armadillo.

The terrain for the most part is extremely rugged. Buckvines, saw briers, and dense undergrowth combine in the swampland, making it exceptionally hard to keep pace with the dogs. It's perfect cover for the game and quite naturally handicaps the hunter. This is the big reason that we never dismount unless we're sure a hog is dead.

"Old Granddad," the hog Ed mentioned as we saddled our horses, was a status symbol in Bourgere. For five years we had been trying to get the old swamp king in our sights, but the old porkster had proven his supremacy time and time again.

He wasn't a large boar, as boar in this particular swamp go, but his wits were as tall as the picturesque and moss-limbed cypress trees that sprinkled his domain. Old 'Dad, as we came to term him, carried his share of combat scars, scars that readily attested to his coveted title as king of the swamp. Over the years, along with our respect, the old rooter had gained the equal respect of the dogs and the horses. The better dogs of the pack gave him all the ground he wanted, and our mounts kept a constant eye on the vicious and beady-eyed little warrior.

Our line of departure today was the Deer Park hunting-fishing lodge. Most folks know it as simply "Jughead's Place." It's located 16 miles down-levee from Vidalia and it is the hub of fishing and hunting activities for the western half of Bourgere Swamp. Completely modern (with the exception of telephones; Jughead says he don't need 'em), the comfortable lodge is situated on the banks of Old River, and is famous for large and tasty servings of catfish and hushpuppies. Of all his wisdom, especially in the outdoor realm, Ed's most guarded secret is the ingredients for the most mouth-watering hushpuppies in the Southland.

As we turned our backs to the biting early October wind and started into the misty swamp, I dared not miss a chance to reminisce a little about the old hog we were after. I even remembered the first time I had seen a sign of the old razorback. "C'mere boy," Ed had yelled. "Let me show you a real hog track." As he dismounted he continued, "Don't look at the size of the track, look at how deep it is cut into the earth. There, my little buddy, is Old Granddad's track, and every time we jump him you just remember that he'd just as soon cut you in two as root up an acorn."

I had thought that Ed was overdoing it just a wee bit, perhaps trying to make the chase sound a little more spicy and dangerous than it really was. But that was my first hunt, and I needed all the advice I could come by.

Before the year was over, however, I found the rooter was all man, and even more dangerous and vicious than Ed had led me to believe.

We saw the old man at least several times a year, but he never presented himself in such a manner as to afford us with a clean, telling shot. His usual routine was to make tracks for the nearest bunch of sows and pigs, mix 'em up real good, and head for deep country while the dogs were trying to straighten the trail out. This method worked for five years.

I had promised Ed on our first hunt that I would stick by his rules in the woods, rules that he rigidly enforced at all times and at all costs. "First and foremost," he explained, "don't cripple 'em. We'll have another day, so let's don't maim our game and let them wander off into the bowels of Bourgere and die." Ed was an ardent hunter and wanted game, but his respect for conservation and the humane manner in which he took it made my respect for him grow by leaps and bounds.

A small ironwood tree limb that Jim had held for quite some time brought me back to reality with a smart lash on my icy nose. "You could have held that limb a little longer, Jim," I yelled through watery eyes, but my retort was lost in the sloosh of the horses tromping through the swampy mire.

A misty fog covered the swamp today, despite the chilling wind. A lazy blue crane left its lofty treetop perch, apparently disturbed at being denied his early morning nap....A woodduck gave out with an eerie squeal as he took wing from a pothole nearby....Shortly after, a swamp rabbit darted between Jim's horse and mine. One of the puppies barked sharply at an armadillo—the extent of the excitement for the next few minutes.

The silence was short-lived. Old Black, the undisputed king of the pack, broke it with a trail bark to our left. "That hog is moving, fellas," Jughead offered. "Wouldn't be worth our time to wait for 'em to bay." We moved on, ever deeper into the thickening undergrowth of the vast swampland.

"Where's the hogs, Ed?" I asked from the rear of the party. "Devils are holed up just now," replied Ed. "They'll be out for an acorn later on, though, don't worry." The small party lapsed back into silence.

Old Black's next signal told us he had bayed to our rear and left. Jim was the first to take rein and make tracks for the arena. Tony, my mount, and I were having a little rein trouble. The left bridle strap was broken, and he was "hellbent for election" to be the first horse to get the bay. With one rein, the task of getting him there, with me still on board, was one that I shall never forget. A saw briar caught me squarely in the mouth, ripping skin and flesh. I felt the sting of several good limb-beatings before I arrived just seconds after Jim. Warm blood oozed down my neck from the deep scratches and my legs ached all over, an aftermath of Tony's taking the trees too close.

The scars healed quickly, however, when I sighted two extremely large boar at bay. Old Black had gained the assurance of the entire pack now, and the dogs were surrounding the rooters in an effort to keep them from breaking bay.

Jim quietly slid from his saddle, shouldered his .222 rifle, took careful aim and squeezed off his first shot. One of the porksters dropped in his tracks. The other, however, took offense, and made a very straight and very deadly charge for Jim.

A small tree four feet from Jim proved to be his blessing in disguise. In one fast movement, and I do mean fast, he dropped his weapon to the ground and made the bottom limb of the tree, but not before the vicious boar had ripped a small piece of his hunting trousers in an attempt to cut him down to size.

Old Black, meanwhile, had come to the rescue, however late. He stood his ground between Jim and the boar long enough for Jim to recover his rifle. Squatting to shoot under a small tree, Jim brought the other hog down with no trouble. His close call was quickly forgotten in the excitement of the kill. "Well now," he boasted, "one of these rooters' heads isn't going to look bad at all on my den wall." He was right, of course. The mounted head of either of them would make a wonderful wall trophy and topic of conversation for years to come.

"It's a pity we don't have the pickup," mused Ed. "We could take these two out and keep right on hunting." Ed was remembering warmer and less watery winter months of years gone by when we were fortunate enough to get his small pickup into the swamp to haul the boar out.

"We're two hours deep now," Ed informed us. "If we turn back now, we'll just about make it in time for a king-sized serving of catfish and hushpuppies."

Richer by almost 900 pounds of pork, now loaded on Ed and Jim's horses, we reined toward home. "Let's swing out to our left," instructed Ed. "Maybe we'll hit paydirt again before we get in." I wasn't too interested in sharing my saddle with a dead boar, but knew that I would if necessary.

The dogs looked hopefully toward deeper country, but resigned themselves to back-tracking and trotted along behind the horses for the first several minutes. Old Black, who usually flanked our left, stayed well behind the horses for some strange reason. His usual desire for wild hogs seemed to disappear.

"Here's a fresh wallow," yelled Jack, our black guide. From the rear of the foursome, it looked real fresh. I watched Old Black out of the corner of my eye as he approached it. As I reined Tony to a stop, the dog sniffed one time and bounded off into the underbrush with his nose high in the air. Seconds later, he bayed, and the other dogs moved in for the hold. Tony meanwhile needed no rein signal from me. Black's bay bark had barely died when Tony whirled and started for the bay. Ed and Jim yelled something about "small pigs" as I veered off into the brush. Had Ed known what was on the other end of this particular bay, he would have dropped his pork load and been the first to arrive.

As I broke the small clearing where Old Black stood, I dared not even hope that this grizzly rooter I was about to face would be Granddad. But there he was, big as life and twice as dangerous. His beady little eyes never left Old Black a moment, until a puppy ventured in too close. The puppy, unaware of the master that he was facing, made the mistake of edging too close. In one swift flash of frothy mouth, with the unmistakable sound of flesh tearing, the puppy lay dead on the ground. Old Black had started to give aid to the puppy, but realizing he was too late, braked to a stop and stayed clear of the vicious hog.

Granddad squared himself toward Old Black now, but the charge never materialized. Black knew what he was facing, and wanted no part of this creature by himself.

As I pulled my rifle from the holster, his eyes flashed toward me for a split second. I tried to read some sort of plea for mercy, but there was none.

106

The greying razorback was asking for nothing. Pity wasn't part of his game. He wanted to die like he had lived.

Five years of intense desire to kill him left me then, and my trigger finger faltered. Should I take the life of this old warrior?

I squeezed the mist from my eyes and the trigger at the same time. The old fella dropped to one knee, then to the other, sank to the earth of Bourgere and died.

The shot brought Ed and Jim to the scene, Ed cussing at having missed the chance of polishing off Old Granddad, and Jim marvelling at the size of the wound that killed the puppy. "This here ain't right at all," Ed bellowed. "Hell's fire, this hog ain't never run a hundred feet and stopped. Seems like the old rascal just wanted to get killed today."

I went over Ed's statement time and time again as we made our way back to the lodge, with the old swamp king sharing my saddle.

Why had he run only a few hundred feet and stopped? Why had he not raced to his harem of sows and pigs, as he had many times in the past? Why had he not made at least some effort toward saving his skin? Last of all, why had I been the one to kill him?

Now, a year later, these questions have been answered, at least to my own satisfaction. Granddad was old....getting older every day. His combat scars alone would have killed any other hog in the swamp. Too, he wasn't as wiry as he was back in his younger days. I think he just picked that day to end his conquest of Bourgere Swamp. Had he picked Ed as his conqueror, he might still be alive, and "next best" to some other hog in the woods. I don't really know, but I can't make myself believe that Old Granddad would have wanted it that way at all. I won't ever know for sure. It's a secret that Granddad carried to his end, and one that Bourgere Swamp will eternally keep.

RESOLUTION TO A HUNTER'S WIFE

Ronnie Strickland

Ronnie Strickland, Natchez, is the field representative for Mossy Oak Camouflage. He is the Outdoor Columnist for the Natchez Democrat *as well as a hunting video producer and cameraman.*

For all you devoted deer hunters that spend more time scouting out that trophy buck than picking out the perfect Christmas gift for your wife, this article is for you. Read it carefully, pick out what you consider the high points, and re-write them in your handwriting. Then leave the note laying where your better half is sure to see it.

The subject of this article is New Year's Resolutions. After another long hunting season, a few good promises to your spouse can have a teriffic effect on your home life.

First, I am assuming you have laid all the needed groundwork for these resolutions to sink in. For example, I hope you have told your wife from the beginning that hunting is hard work, and the only reason you do it is to put meat on the table. Never let on that you enjoy shooting the bull with the guys at the deer camp, shooting your bow for hours on end, riding your ATV every week-end while looking for deer sign, or building tree stands in August instead of mowing the lawn. Tell her that all you do in the woods is for the good of the family, and it truly is lots of hard work.

Next, start your New Years Resolutions list with a note of thanks—for instance: Thank you ever so much for putting up with all the little inconveniences that go along with living with an outdoorsman; for all the mornings you wake up at 4:00 a.m. when the clock sounds off, for listening to my buddies' hunting and fishing stories with interest when I'm not home, for cooking all types of wild game and acting like you enjoyed it even if you didn't, and for feeding my prize black lab when I sometimes was too busy to stop.

After the list of thanks is complete, you can now start listing your resolutions if you dare. One important note here—never list a resolution without an excuse following. The excuse must be a good one, and will keep you from looking like more of a heel than you already do at times.

Let me offer some examples:

I will try to do less turkey hunting this spring so I can carry the kids to school each morning unless I get in that new hunting club that is loaded with long beards.

I will spend less time at the archery range unless I manage to buy that new bow I've been wanting for two years.

I promise not to hunt between the end of deer season in January and turkey season in March unless old so-and-so asks me to join him on a rabbit hunt with his prize beagles.

I promise our vacation to Colorado won't be during the hunting season unless I get drawn for a permit to hunt section 64.

I promise no shooting my bow from the roof of the house while the neighbors are walking around the block unless that new tree stand sight gives me trouble again this year.

I promise not to fall asleep on the couch at 7:00 p.m. every night during spring turkey season especially when you have company, unless that old gobbler on White Oak ridge is still alive.

I promise not to buy you another gun for Christmas next year unless the sports shop gets in one of those new Remington model sevens in a 243 caliber.

I promise not to run out of the house right after Thanksgiving dinner to hunt during the afternoon unless I did not kill a buck that morning.

I promise not to wear camouflage clothing to any social event this year while in your company unless some of the boys may be there.

I promise not to leave any more dead critters in the refrigerator without warning you first unless you and the taxidermist are out of pocket.

Toward the end of your New Years Resolution list, mention that you will try to catch up on all your honey-do's. You might go as far as to tell your loving wife to update her list of honey-do's so that you don't overlook anything she may need done around the house.

If your wife is like mine, she will most likely know that most of these promises, along with the honey-do list, will get far less attention than your hunting camp, hunting buddies, hunting and fishing equipment, or your daydreams. If she has been putting up with you for very long, she is for all practical purposes part angel and part dinosaur. She is an absolute God-send and there are not many like her around. Take care of her and do let her know that she is more precious to you than your best trophy head; and never forget—hunting is hard work.

THE MARRIAGE OF A DEER HUNTER

Jim McCafferty

Larry Webster stood on the front steps of the little Baptist church on the south end of New Albany. He shifted his weight from foot to foot to keep the blood circulating and to ward off the late December chill. He glanced at his watch. Two p.m. It would be another hour before the rest of the crowd began to arrive, he supposed. But he was a deer hunter, and he was accustomed to being early.

Larry was not entirely happy about being at the church on this wintery Saturday afternoon. During the night the wind had shifted to the northwest, and the sky had filled with leaden clouds. The mercury had dropped 20 points since he got up, and the light mist that was falling during the morning was beginning to change to fine sleet. The deer out in the national forest would be moving, trying to get a few last meals in their bellies before the ice and snow arrived, and Larry would have much preferred to have been sneaking along a certain logging road he knew. He had seen a big buck along that trail a few evenings back, and.....

But he had no choice today. For now it would have to be a rented tux and patent leather shoes for Larry Webster, not the camouflage coveralls and L. L. Bean hunting boots that were usually his uniform on days like this one. Today, Chris Webster, his only child and heir at law, was to be married.

That, too, caused Larry more than just a little concern. It was not that he was against the marriage. He could not have picked a better mate for his Chris had he done it himself. He was just a little afraid; afraid that

111

a part of his life was slipping away from him and might soon be gone forever.

Larry and Chris did not have the typical parent-child relationship. Larry had lost his wife to illness just a few months after Chris was born. Aunts and other female kin had offered to help rear the child, but Larry had refused. Chris was his child: his responsibility. Those relatives had their doubts about a young man's ability to take on the job of raising a baby single-handedly, Larry recalled. But now, 23 years later, no one in New Albany could find any fault with the way his Chris had turned out.

They had come through all the stages together: the first steps, the first words, the first days at school. But of all his memories, Larry most treasured his recollections of the times he and Chris had spent in the woods.

A panel truck pulled up in front of the church, interrupting Larry's reminiscing. The driver got out, and Larry recognized him as the delivery boy for the florist. "I'm running a little late with some of the greenery for the wedding, Mr. Webster," the boy said.

"No problem," Larry replied, "there's still plenty of time." The delivery boy passed with an armload of evergreen boughs. The fresh pine scent triggered something in the back of his brain, and his thoughts again drifted to Chris and the deer woods.

He recalled the first deer Chris had ever seen. Chris could not have been more than four or five years old. The two had been out one September Saturday for a walk in the woods. Larry was scouting for the upcoming bow season; Chris was along for the ride. Sensing that his little one was getting tired, Larry stopped for a breather along the side of a pine-covered ridge. They had been there for only a minute or two when the buck appeared from nowhere in the bottom below. Chris saw him first. "Look at the pony, Daddy," the child had said. It was an easy mistake to make, for the deer was a monster. Larry signaled Chris to be still. For only a moment the buck stood frozen, staring toward their position on the hillside. He was a handsome animal, with a chest like a beer keg, and a full, heavy rack. Larry counted nine points before the buck galloped over the next ridge and out of sight.

Larry was impressed, but not half so much as Chris. For the next month the pre-schooler bombarded Larry with questions about deer: "Where do they sleep? How old do they get?" Chris wanted to know everything there was to know about white-tails. And to Larry's delight, the most frequently asked question was, "When can I go deer hunting with you, Daddy?"

No doubt about it, Larry had a fledgling deer hunter on his hands. The next few years rushed by like a freight train. Almost before Larry knew it, Chris was about to turn 13. "Think of that," Larry caught himself muttering one day at work, "I'm going to be the father of a teenager."

When the big day arrived, Larry left work early and met Chris at school. They drove downtown to the Western Auto Store where Larry had a surprise waiting. "A .30-.30!" Chris squealed, shouldering the brand new Winchester.

"It's just the right size for you now," Larry remarked, "but you're growing faster than a set of deer antlers. By next season you're bound to need a new stock. But we'll worry about that when the time comes. Right now you've got to start practicing. It's only two months until the first gun season."

And practice Chris did. The gun took a little getting used to. It was louder and heavier than the .22's Chris had shot, and the .30-caliber cartridges kicked almost too hard for a skinny 13-year-old's shoulder. Larry winced each time the youngster touched off a round. But Chris never complained, and by the Saturday before opening day, that Winchester was punching out bulls-eyes at 100 yards.

The last week before the beginning of that first season must have been the longest seven days in Chris' young life, Larry thought. Early each morning before school that week the two of them would drive the 30 miles to their chosen hunting area near Chewalla Creek in Holly Springs National Forest for some last-minute scouting. With each trip Chris grew more and more excited. By Friday, the teenager's enthusiasm had begun to affect Larry. He tossed and turned that night for what seemed like weeks, and when the alarm went off at 3:30 a.m., he felt as if he hadn't slept at all. No matter; he rose quickly and dressed. "Guess I'd better wake Chris," he said to himself, still half asleep. As he stepped out into the hall, the deliciously familiar smell of coffee and frying bacon told him that Chris had already been up for some time.

After breakfast, Larry and Chris got into the truck for the drive to Holly Springs National Forest. They were quiet most of the way; something about the pre-dawn stillness outside the pick-up seemed to discourage too much talking. Larry parked the old Ford about a half-mile from the area they had targeted for their morning hunt. Chris quietly opened the passenger-side door. "Daddy, look at those stars. They look close enough to touch," the youngster whispered.

Larry looked skyward. Deep in the woods, far from the lights of New Albany and Holly Springs, the stars took on a special brilliance rarely seen by house-bound city dwellers. As a deer hunter, of course, Larry had been treated to that spectacle over and over again. Still, each time he saw that sparkling winter sky, his reaction was the same: complete and overwhelming awe. For Larry, the hunt was already a success.

Chris and Larry tied on their hunter orange and pocketed a dozen rounds of ammunition each. "Meet me back here at ten," Larry said. Chris nodded, and disappeared into the dark.

Thanks to many hours of scouting, both hunters were intimately familiar with the sections of the forest they would be hunting. Chris had previously selected a spot on the side of a cut-over ridge overlooking a small clearing in an otherwise heavily wooded, swampy creek bottom. Any deer using the well-traveled trail through the swamp would have to show itself briefly in the clearing, offering an alert hunter a shot. Larry stationed himself along the same ridge, about 600 yards up the hollow from Chris.

With more than an hour remaining until legal shooting time, both hunters were already settled down at their stands. Larry worried a little about his young companion. Would Chris have the patience to sit still all morning in the November chill? Or would the cold and the solitude prove too much for the 13-year-old.

The dawn was only a minute or two old when Larry heard the shot. There was a short silence, followed by an Indian war whoop that would have done justice to Geronimo. Double-timing it down the hollow, Larry found Chris standing over a healthy, six-point buck, shot cleanly through the lungs.

Chris looked ready to come apart with pride and excitement. "He's a big one, isn't he, Dad! I'll bet he weighs 250 pounds!" Larry knew the deer probably weighed closed to 150, but he just nodded his head. "He's a big one, all right, Chris. Now stand still for a second and be quiet. I've got something important to do." Chris, a little confused, obeyed.

Larry brushed his hand over the fresh wound in the buck's chest. He then rubbed the same hand across Chris's face, smearing the deer's hot blood across the youngster's cheeks.

Chris drew back. "Why are you doing that?" Chris asked.

"It's an old Chickasaw custom," Larry answered solemnly. "It means you are a hunter, that you respect the blood you have spilled."

A warm glow filled Chris's eyes, and in his child's face Larry saw everything that he had ever hoped for. How proud he was of his young hunter! "I would rather spend time out here with this kid than anything," he thought.

Over the next several years, finding time to spend together became harder and harder for Chris and Larry. Chris's world became filled with all those things that occupy a teenager's time. There were church functions, athletics, and, of course, dating.

Larry's schedule likewise grew more complex. Promotions at the plant brought increased responsibilities, which meant more overtime. But he didn't mind that so much, since it also meant extra money. With Chris approaching college age, he needed all the money he could get.

Each winter, though, busy or not, Larry and Chris reserved their Saturdays for themselves. And, with each deer season that passed, Larry added to his inventory of happy memories of times shared with Chris. There was Chris's first deer taken with a bow, the big ten-point Chris got with a muzzle-loader. The list went on and on.

Now, though, Larry feared it was all coming to an end. Marriage brought unavoidable changes into a young person's life. Larry knew that. There would be dozens of new responsibilities competing for Chris's time: new jobs, household duties, maybe even children. And, as Larry knew from the experience of some of his friends at work, some spouses objected to their marriage partners "wasting" time hunting. Would Chris have that problem? "If so, it will be my problem, too," Larry sadly realized.

Another car stopped in front of the church. This one Larry recognized immediately. The driver's door opened and out stepped the only

116

child of Larry Webster. He had never seen Chris look brighter or happier, and for a moment, Larry forgot his gloomy thoughts.

"You're early, Chris," Larry said.

"I know. But I'm a deer hunter. I'm used to it." They walked up the steps and through the tall double doors of the church. They paused for a few moments in the dark vestibule, and Larry again found his thoughts turning melancholy.

"What's wrong, Dad?" asked Chris.

"Nothing."

"Come on, you can't fool me. We've been together too long."

Against his better judgment, Larry confessed what was on his mind. Chris smiled. "I'm not about to run out on you now, Dad. Our days together are just beginning. Come on, now, we've got to start moving. Other people are beginning to show up."

The next 60 minutes passed like so many seconds. Larry, reassured by Chris' words, was ready to joyously perform his role in the upcoming ceremony. At last, the moment arrived. As the organist began the first strains of the Wedding March, Larry took his deer hunter's arm in his own and stepped through the vestibule door into the aisle of the crowded church. "Chris," he whispered, as they walked toward the altar, "you're the finest daughter that a man ever had."

KAYAK ADVENTURE

Ernest Herndon

Black Creek is one of the South's finest streams. It flows through jumbled southeastern Mississippi bluffs with cold groundwater seeping through the striated clay, past walls of looming forest. In the meantime it passes through the DeSoto National Forest, including the Black Creek Wilderness, en route to its covergence first with Red Creek and then with the Pascagoula River.

The Pascagoula is a horse of a different color. Wide. Muddy. Swampish. With a sweet stink reminiscent of beaver caster and aged muck. Braided with dead rivers, ox-bow lakes and bayous, the Pascagoula crawls toward the Gulf of Mexico, fanning out into vast salt marshes before oozing into the Mississippi Sound in a welter of mosquitoes and marsh grass.

Years ago Henry David Thoreau wrote *A Week On The Concord And Merrimack Rivers*. This was a week on Black Creek and the Pascagoula River. In a kayak. Not always right-side up.

My friend Scott Williams of Prentiss, a 25-year-old with an addiction to adventure who later was to kayak across the Caribbean solo, accompanied me, each of us in a sea kayak.

A sea kayak is much like a whitewater river kayak except it is a bit more stable and spacious and has a rudder. It is fully capable of handling rough seas—though the person inside might not be, as I will attest. This was my first encounter with such a craft. Williams had taken his on jaunts as far out as Horn Island in the Mississippi Sound, 12 miles offshore.

118

We put in at Brooklyn, Mississippi, one fine autumn afternoon, loaded with gear and ready to spend a week paddling 100-odd miles to the sea. Drifting down a river the color of iced tea, for days we were to hear nary a human sound and see no one.

The river runs between broad sand bars and high bluffs with springs tumbling from the clay banks. We paddled without a care, stopping to sip spring water, nibble M&M's, swim, nap in the shade, and read—I in my *Week On Concord* etc.

Paddling a kayak is work, mind you. It gets to your shoulders, arms and back. You get cramped up sitting in the little cockpit. But by Wednesday afternoon, our fourth day, we were in the rhythm of paddling. We'd been traveling in a lazy, hypnotic trance, dazzled by sunlight, shade, and late September breezes.

At the bridge on Highway 57, we directed the 16-foot boats to the muddy bank and climbed out to stretch our cramped muscles. It was 3:30 p.m. We had been paddling since 9:30 that morning.

We seemed to be running behind schedule. We had left Sunday with intentions of reaching the Gulf of Mexico in seven days. Yet here it was Wednesday and we were still a long way from the Pascagoula. There seemed to be just one solution: paddle straight on through to the big river without stopping.

There was no hope of reaching it by dark. Judging by our maps, we had a good 15-20 miles of creek ahead of us. Off we went.

As we plowed down the river, it grew wider, muddier, and slower. Soon we saw more cypress trees than pines, and Spanish moss dangled over the current. Trees arched overhead in a jungle canopy.

We stopped once to get water from a spring, and swamp mosquitoes jumped us.

Williams doused himself with Avon Skin So Soft, said to be the best mosquito repellent going. The problem is—with all due respect to clients seeking softer skin—it stinks.

"You smell like a floating house of ill repute," I told Williams, though not so daintily. We raced for the privilege of being upwind.

As it got dark, navigating among the logs and submerged branches became intuitive. Overhanding limbs blocked the dusklight. We had to respond to wisps of shadow and glimmers of light on the surface of the river.

The water exploded just ahead of me like a cannonshot. I jumped, then chuckled. Beaver, more scared than I. Probably cruising along and glanced up to see a big, silent kayak bearing down on him.

I noticed what appeared to be a log in front of the boat. As I neared, it sank without a sound or ripple and did not resurface. Only one thing that could be: alligator.

In the blackness I detected a shadow and moved my head to the left. Dangling branches zipped by.

There seemed to be some gray mass up ahead. Before I had time to investigate, my kayak slammed head-on into a tree which had fallen across the river. The current swept me sideways against the log. I heaved the boat forward hoping to find a passage, but rammed another log.

Behind me Williams stopped when he heard my commotion and pulled out a flashlight. You can't very well hold a flashlight and wield a double-bladed kayak paddle at the same time, of course, so we had been relying strictly on night vision.

Williams' light showed the river blocked by the fallen tree. While he played his beam over it, I kept a watch on the network of branches caressing my shoulder. They looked a bit snaky. The current was pressing the boat hard against the tree. This would be no place to flip.

120

Williams found a way through, a two-foot-wide opening just past the treetop. By main force I dragged my boat out of its predicament, and we continued.

After we reached the convergence of Red and Black Creeks, the river broadened and we didn't have to worry too much about snags. The moon, just past full, rose over the water, and screech owls talked in the language of the swamp. Side by side in silence we plied our kayaks down the broad, moonstruck river through the black forest toward the wide Pascagoula.

By midnight-30 we were doggone miserable. We had reached the Pascagoula, and there was nowhere to pitch a tent, nothing but mud and jungle and high bluffs.

The river was wide and bright under the nearly full moon. Up ahead was a narrow sand flat exposed by low water. It was a dangerous place to camp—the slightest rise in water would flood it—but after 15 hours of paddling we were too tired to care. We pitched a tent on the wet sand and hauled our boats well away from the water's edge.

"We're okay as long as it doesn't rain," I said.

I fell asleep once I made Williams quit snoring. I had nightmares of flooding rivers and sat up wide-eyed, still asleep, with thunder cracking all around. Staring out of the tent, I hallucinated a flooding river. I stuck my hand outside the mosquito netting to see if the water was up to the tent, and mosquitoes glommed onto my hand in dozens. I yanked it back in and zipped the netting shut. The river wasn't up yet.

Shortly after daylight a hard rain hit. The river was inching up. We dragged our boats closer to the tent, marked the water's edge with a stick, and fell back asleep.

We finally paddled away from camp in the late morning under a cold drizzle.

Ah, Pascagoula River! I've never smelled anything quite like it, and I hope I don't again any time soon. The river looks about half the size of the Mississippi and has plenty of mud and few sand bars. Yet it has its surprises.

A clean, graceful waterfall tumbled four feet down a clay bank. When I went over to investigate, mosquitoes ambushed me. Welted with bites and speckled with blood, I jumped back in my kayak and paddled out to mid-river where the breeze blew them away.

Despite the vastness of the swamp, the Pascagoula River did not feel as remote as Black Creek had. In the distance was the grind of machinery, and vacant, floating fishermen's camps were tied to the banks near landings. Yet once we paddled past Highway 614, there were to be no more bridges until we reached Interstate 10 some 30 river miles south.

The Pascagoula splits into an east river and a west river, and we took the west fork, said to be more scenic. Here the river was truly a swamp. It scarcely flowed at all, and was lined with dense cypress woods and swamp grass.

As it grew dark we were fortunate to find a mud flat in a sharp bend, and cooked supper under a sunset the color of a brand-new silver-blue Buick.

It didn't take long the next day to reach marsh country, miles of marsh grass and serpentine bayous. Drivers on I-10 over the Pascagoula River get a good aerial view of this huge wetland. Relying on maps, we took a shortcut through the maze of bayous, passed under the interstate and rejoined the main river. From there it was a hard pull against the wind on big water down to Highway 90 at the mouth of the river where the town of Pascagoula sits. We arrived a day earlier than expected.

"Let's paddle out to Round Island," Williams said.

Why not?

The island, a half-mile-long wedge of sand and pine trees with an abandoned lighthouse at one end, lies two and a half miles out in the Mississippi Sound. We agreed to journey out to the deserted isle, spend the night, and return to Pascagoula.

I had never paddled in open seas, but Williams figured the water was protected enough from the open Gulf by barrier islands to be safe. He gave me brief instructions in handling waves and in climbing back into the kayak in the extremely unlikely event we capsized. And we were off to sea.

It was thrilling to paddle out to open sea in a 16-foot-long, two-and-a-half-foot-wide plastic boat. I felt like a beer commercial hero, ready for all the gusto I could grab.

The seas got choppier as we left the protection of the mainland, and once we passed the last little marshy islet the water gave our boats a tossing.

A sea kayak is far sturdier than it looks. Completely enclosed, it floats on the water like an elongated cork, and big splashing waves have little effect on it. A spray skirt around the waist helps keep water out, and a dry compartment in the stern adds buoyancy.

I felt as bold as a puppy stepping into the yard for the first time as we entered the mile-and-a-half open stretch en route to the island. Out in the sound ahead of us I saw whitecaps as a 15-knot southeast wind whipped the sea up.

I pulled up alongside Williams, chatted a moment, then grabbed my second wind and pulled ahead. It was great to be in an invulnerable boat! After a week of paddling, my arms, shoulders and back felt strong and sure.

I heard Williams' emergency whistle and looked back, but he just waved so I kept paddling. He whistled again, and this time he motioned frantically for me to stop. He pulled up.

"I'm taking water bad," he said. "I'm sinking!"

His boat rode sickeningly low in the water, with waves lapping around his waist. I felt a breath of pure fear.

"Hand me that bilge pump," he said, and I yanked it loose from my boat and handed it to him, bracing our kayaks together as he began pumping furiously. "You can pull away now," he said.

I pulled to the right, leaning as I did, and got caught broadside by a big wave. That's when I discovered that the underside of the Mississipi Sound is a sort of amber-green in color.

My boat had flipped. I thrashed wildly with my legs and came loose, surfacing in the turbulent sea.

It wasn't a joke any more and it wasn't fun. I was capsized, Williams was sinking, three-foot waves were pounding us, and I had a bellyful of seawater.

I held to the side of my rollicking, now-full craft as Williams paddled over. I tried not to think of sharks lured by the frantic kick of my legs in the murky green water. He pumped and I bailed to get some water out of my boat, then he suggested I get back in.

Getting back in a kayak is tricky business. You're supposed to clamber up with your belly down on the back of your boat facing the stern, slip your feet into the cockpit, and turn and slide in all at the same time. The sort of thing a Soviet gymnast would be good at.

I gave a try and the boat flipped back over. A moment's exhaustion made me realize I wouldn't have many chances.

"Maybe you can stabilize yourself on my boat," Williams said.

There was an unhappy look in his eyes as he braced his own wallowing craft next to mine against the brunt of the waves. I pulled myself around the stern of my boat and climbed onto his as though it were a supermarket horse. Then I slipped over onto mine, belly-down on the stern, slid my legs in, turned and went in.

124

Thank you, God.

Now I was back in my boat, but my boat was full of water. I grabbed the bilge pump and went to work.

"Better put your spray skirt on first," Williams warned.

What did he know? But just as I got a good bit pumped out, a wave filled the boat again. I fastened down the spray skirt in a hurry. Williams held the boats steady while I pumped until my right arm gave out, pumped until my left gave out, then switched back to the right. Suddenly the pump clogged. My raincoat, loose in the boat, was jamming it. I yanked the coat out and tossed it to the seas. Never liked the color of it anyway. Sort of an off-maroon. Next some old khaki pants stopped it. They were always too baggy. I chunked them.

Finally I got three-fourths of the water out, thanked God heartily, and gave the pump back to Williams, who resumed trying to save his own craft. Meanwhile the wind had blown us probably half a mile off course, away from Round Island. We began the toilsome work of paddling against the wind. Periodically Williams had to stop and pump. He was riding low and heavy.

By the time we made it to the lee of the island we were exhausted, and I was sick from my seawater cocktail. We replaced our prayers for salvation with prayers of gratitude when the hulls struck sand.

That night we camped on the beach and watched the lights of Pascagoula compete with the stars while the wind whipped across the Gulf of Mexico. We sat in the sand and talked quietly, slapping no-see-ums and absorbing the ocean breeze. Later, as we slept, a sudden, hard-driving rainstorm nearly blew us and our tent away, and then all was still again.

At dawn the sun was out, the breeze down, and the water smooth and gentle. Williams found the leak in his boat and patched it with duct tape, which should hold if the seas weren't too rough. We loaded the boats, studied the waves, tested the wind. We wanted assurance.

Finally, we decided we were ready. We were nervous, it was true, but we pushed off from Round Island into a calm sea, under a pleasant sun, with the lightest of breezes trickling over us now and then to soothe our labors.

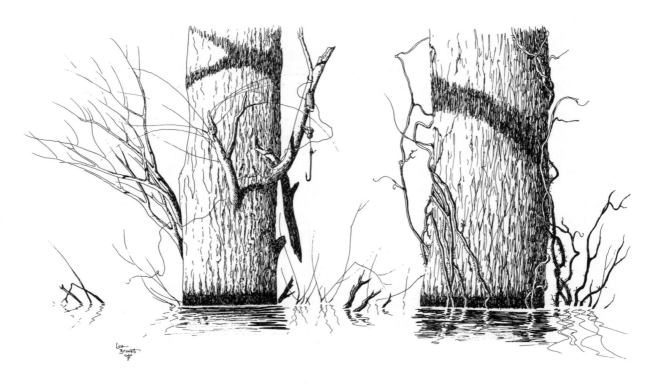

126

Lisa Brunetti

JONES COUNTY COTTONTAILS

John Woods

John J. Woods, Hattiesburg, is the coordinator of a Mississippi State University Extension Center. He is also Contributing Editor for North American Hunter, The Rabbit Hunter, *and* The Panfisherman *magazines. He free-lances for several other magazines, as well.*

When you decide to take up the sport of rabbit hunting, you quickly find out that, like other outdoor sports, you just don't always get the cards dealt to you right. Sometimes the weather fails you, sometimes it's bad dogs, other times your favorite shotgun may let you down, or maybe a drive shaft parts company from your truck. I've had all these things happen while rabbit hunting, and "it don't make for no picnic," as they say.

But then again, you flip that coin over, and the other side looks pretty bright. The hunting grounds are just damp enough to give a good scent trail, the dogs are perky and ready to run, and well, everything just goes right for a change. We finally pulled off one of those kinds of hunts just before the season lapsed for another year.

Of course, you can always control who you hunt with, and on that given day we had quite a troupe. The hunt was organized by the ole Moselle beagle handler himself, Max Phillips, and his son, Macon. Along for the chase besides myself were friends Jack Busby, Jim and Trent Harris, Charles Garretson, and a rabbit slayer named Neil Walters.

Now Mississippi doesn't get a lot of cold weather, but along about February, residents can expect a little weather that northern folks would term "nippy". The thermometer this day was hovering around 39 degrees with a steady breeze. Rain was a definite possibility, given strong odds by the local weather forecasts.

When we arrived at the Phillips' hunt headquarters, Max's sweet darlin' of a wife had a king's breakfast on the table gettin' cold. I'll assure you it didn't take long for our bunch to reduce her efforts to a pile of dirty dishes. Miss June makes biscuits that would drive an honest man to leave home. But I doubt Max would let me move in. Truth be known, the only reason we go on Max's beagle chases in the first place is for June's cooking and hospitality. This family rates No. 1 in my book.

We broke off the feed, saddled up the wagons, boxed the dogs, and headed out. About a half dozen miles from Max's house lies one of the meanest hilly pine cutovers you ever laid eyes on. Allowed to grow up for about three years after a replant, the place was exceptional rabbit habitat. The terrain was tough going down in the bottoms, but nothing stopped the dogs.

We got parked and settled, and released the beagles to do their morning stretches and constitutionals. Max allowed a few minutes to give us the layout of the property and a rough plan for covering as much ground as possible. Of course, that's usually dictated by what the dogs do. This hunt was not to be an exception to that rabbit-hunting principle.

Within just a few minutes, the pack struck a hot trail, and we were off and running. Part of the land had rather smooth terrain, but was grown up in head high weeds. The owner had gone in weeks before and bushhogged wide walkways all through the weeded sections. This allowed the hunter a clear walking space, and gave the dogs a place to chase a rabbit into the openings.

The initial chase led us down into a draw that was a literal tangle of mess. If you've ever seen a timbered cutover, then you know what I'm talking about. The area looked like a scene from a Vietnam War bomb zone. The ground was littered with tree branches, pushed-over saplings, and all manner of twisted leftover tree residue. What a grand place for rabbits indeed!

It wasn't long until this action produced a couple of bunnies for the bag. Since I was toting my camera along with my shotgun, I had an excuse for not getting to bust a primer. The others took care of that. Max and his beagle band worked that cutover for nearly an hour. We got several good runs out of it. Whenever the dogs bogged down, Max was on the spot urging them on to new thickets. Max rates high as a beagle task master.

The dogs kept us on a round-robin hunt. We'd be down in the draws one minute, and then up top the next. Nearly everyone that wanted to brave the briars got in some good rabbit-hunting action. A couple of times I could swear ole Neil or Charlie were poised to shoot themselves in the foot. When a rabbit darts by, you had better not tarry, because they won't give you much leeway for a shot.

As the hunt progressed toward noon, the heavy overcast kept trying to spit out some cold rain, but the rabbit hunter gods must have been smiling on us as the rain held off. We broke for lunch, and Macon made a grocery run back to the house for grub and fresh dogs. As the commercial on TV says, "Boys, it don't get any better than this." I doubt cold Vienna sausages, lunch meat, and saltines ever tasted that good, especially along with a cup of Jack Busby's hot coffee.

We lazed around for a spell trying to regain some warmth and rest up a bit before one more go at an afternoon hunt. The weather and the temp seemed to be holding, so we were forced by popular vote to strike out again. The afternoon action was much a repeat of the morning session with a couple more hides added to the meat sack. We had several more real good runs to cap the day.

About 2:30 in the afternoon, both hunters and dogs were showing signs of tiring, so we elected to call it quits. We rounded up the dogs and headed back to the trucks. In all we had only taken six rabbits, but a couple were of canecutter size. I guess some would not measure this much of a rabbit hunt, but we drew out every bit of hunting fun we could, and I think we all felt the hunt was a good one. I know I did.

The measure of a successful hunt should never be in the count of the game taken anyway. What makes a fine hunt is the companionship of good friends, a bevy of active hunting dogs, some good rabbit chases with dogs mouthing from places below you where no man dare venture, a couple of well-taken shots, and the safe practice of our sport. The Lord gave us all that on our Jones County cottontail hunt for this year. He just threw in the Viennas and soda crackers for good measure.

TRAINING FISH TO HUNT

George D. Warner, Jr.

I hope you read somewhere 'bout the research done at Berkley, the huge fishing outfit. They found out that fish are Super Sniffers. That the nose on fish is so sensitive they can smell and recognize most anything, including man. Why, salmon in a stream can smell a bear if he wades in upstream, and they will scoot! They have learned the bear is danger. He eats 'um. So it is not just their nose—they can remember and identify.

The research folks also found out fish can be trained. We know you train whales and dolphin, but they trained minnows to identify things by smell. Then they made the classical boo-boo. They said fish not only can be trained, but they have a nose better than a hunting dog! Well, that did it. I got me some poop on how to train fish, caught myself 15 minnows, two catfish, three bream and two bass, and went to work. I am now ready to reveal the results of *my* scientific study! Needless to say, you ain't gonna believe this.

First, I bought some Essence of Squirrel, a bottle of Deer Delight, three ounces of Quail Aroma, and some Dove Decoyee. You might have some trouble finding these scents at your favorite store, but look good anyway.

Next I got some sho 'nuff good fish food. I put all the fishes in one tank and did not feed for two days. Then I started drippin' in a microdot of scent. This was done by dippin' a pin point in the scent then dippin' the pin in the tank with the fish. I put a small parcel of fish food by the dipped place. Soon the fish knew if they came to the scent they got fed.

Then I started saying "dove" or "quail" out loud as I dipped. I got kinda dippy, but the fish learned fast. If I said "quail", then gave them a drop of squirrel, they found no food. The game had to match the scent. In one week I had those fish coming only to the scent I called out. Then I was ready.

Opening day of dove season I took a minnow bucket and ten of my best sniffin' hunting minnows into a milo field. To get them keyed up I dropped in a minute drop of Dove Decoyee with some food. Then I just yelled "Dove!" Unreal! Wonderful! Simply unbelievable! When the doves got within 100 yards the minnows turned and faced them. I called for "Singles!" Each minnow pointed to only one dove. That way I could watch the bucket and tell how many doves were comin' in from what direction. Lotsa times all ten minnows were pointing the same way so I swung and tripled on a flight. Great. All the other hunters thought I had some cool drinks. I never let them look in the bucket. They might not of understood and sent me home.

The next day I took one of the bream, put a line on his lip, and went out to the upper end of the Chunky River where it crosses the Super Slabs and is shallow. I put the bream in and walked him like on a leash. All I did was yell "Squirrel!" For two hours it was wild. He would swim along, then suddenly he would come to the top, point with his nose, and wiggle his tail. Sure 'nuff. There would be a squirrel in a tree looking at us. I could have killed a lifetime limit in an hour.

It was kinda hairy at one point. I passed an ole coot bank fishing. He wanted to know what I was doing. When I told him fish hunting he had the most peculiar look on his face. I peculiared back at him and kept on wading.

132

Next I took the two bass. Put them in the minnow bucket and went to a sage field near Scooba. I had only to whisper "Quail," as bass are so smart and have acute hearing. Man alive! I couldn't believe it a'tall. If one bass got a whiff of quail he pointed his snout and moved nary a fin. The other would honor the point! I kicked up a covey and they both held. Then as I walked to find the singles, the bass separated and each would point a different bird. I coulda killed two dozen quail in an hour, but I had to try the Deer Delight.

I took the two catfish in the bucket and went to a soybean field. Climbed up in a deer stand and sat and watched the cats. Nothing! Then I remembered and softly said "Deer." That did it. Both perked up and started sniffin'. In a minute both were looking at a pine clump. Sure 'nuff, here came a nice big doe. Then I looked and both had their fins pointed straight up. I did not understand until out walked a young buck with horns still in the velvet. The darned cats were telling me if it was to be a buck or a doe! The buck started to chase the doe all over the field and finally caught her. I looked and the cats were kissin'!

Now that gave me another idea. Yeah! That will be some sho 'nuff fun running those experiments. A report on fish emotions soon, if I don't pant out.

Get Outdoors!

PEARL RIVER PASSAGE

Bruce Brady

Bruce Brady, Bookhaven, is Editor-at-large for Outdoor Life *magazine, having joined the staff of that publication in 1972. As a wildlife sculptor his work is shown nationwide. He is also the award-winning author of* Game Trails.

The current caught our boat and forced it to the channel side of the river. To keep us off the snaggy shore, Charlie Elliott dug his paddle into the flow and brought us around parallel to the bank. Ahead, the twisted limbs of a fallen oak protruded above the surface.

After putting his paddle down, Charlie shot his bladed lure between the branches of the drowned tree. He retrieved rapidly to clear the limbs, and when his lure fluttered on the surface a bass hammered it. The rod snapped into a tight arc as the fish slashed through the treetop and then burrowed deep toward the tree's tangled roots.

My boatmate pulled the fish away from the bottom into open water and watched it make four acrobatic jumps. Then the fish's steam ran out, and it came in on its side.

"I've caught about every fish there is," my partner said softly, "and these little spotted bass have as much spunk as any."

At my suggestion, he held his fish up for a picture and then eased it gently into the clear water.

134

In Southern waters, bass action begins to slow down by mid-June, but the Pearl River bass apparently hadn't gotten the word. We'd had a busy morning, and the anglers in our companion boat had too.

Five of us were on a two-day float-fishing and camping trip down central Mississippi's Pearl River. Our party was composed of Charlie Elliott, Chet Fish, Bob Stamps, Donald Spence, and myself.

Charlie was Southern Field Editor of *Outdoor Life* magazine and makes his home in Covington, Georgia. Charlie and I have been friends for a number of years, and we've enjoyed some great hunting and fishing trips together.

Chet Fish was Managing Editor of *Outdoor Life* and hailed originally from Massachusetts, but settled in Greenlawn, on Long Island, New York. Chet has an abiding interest in the outdoors. This was his first visit to the Magnolia State.

Bob Stamps and I grew up together in Brookhaven. Bob was 38 and operated a florist shop. He is one of the finest wingshots around, and he's a confirmed bass fisherman.

Donald Spence was 27 and, like his father before him, was reared on the banks of the Pearl River in Lawrence County. Don knows more than 100 miles of the river as intimately as you and I know our backyards. For a good many years he made his living on the river as a commercial fisherman, taxidermist, and trapper, and by digging freshwater mussels for sale to the button industry. Before alligators were protected, he was probably the top gator hunter between Jackson and the Gulf. He also caught snakes of all types for sale to Florida snake farms.

Don had been a game warden for three years. At the conclusion of his second year in the job he was named Warden of the Year by the game and fish commissioners. I've hunted with him. He's an avid bowhunter and at that time had taken more than 20 white-tails with arrows. Part

Choctaw Indian, he moves through the woods like a ghost, and his eyes miss nothing. We looked to him as captain of our expedition.

I was 38, a lawyer and outdoor writer from Brookhaven. My wife, Peg, and I have three children, all of whom have inherited a love for the outdoors.

We'd begun our trip just after daylight that morning when we launched two 16-foot johnboats in the shadow of the Highway 84 bridge east of Monticello. First we ran upstream under power for a few miles. Don was anxious to show Chet and Charlie that section of the river with its high, wooded banks and innumerable springs of fresh, cold water gushing out of the limestone ledges; then too, its bassy water with stumps, snags, rocky ledges, and whole trees fallen into the river.

The Pearl is one of Mississippi's most scenic rivers. It got its name from the rough pearls the Indians found inside the freshwater mussels. It heads in Winston County, pours through the spillways of the dam at the 33,000-acre Ross Barnett Reservoir near Jackson, and slowly wends its way to the Gulf.

As in most big rivers these days, there is pollution in the Pearl. From Jackson southward for a number of miles, industrial and municipal wastes flow into the river. Not until the stream reaches Georgetown in Copiah County does it begin to cleanse itself. The city of Jackson has installed a multimillion-dollar sewage treatment plant, and the day may come when the entire river is free from contamination.

We began our fishing day north of the Monticello bridge. Charlie and I were in the commissary boat, which was loaded to the gunwales with a 9 x 12-foot tent, five sleeping bags and air mattresses, lanterns, cooking gear, and a big grub box. We worked the west bank and left the eastern bank to the other boat.

136

I was watching when Charlie whipped his rubber-skirted spinner past a decaying stump. Nothing happened, so he reeled in and cast to the other side of the stump. As he pumped the lure, a fish jolted it. The fish waltzed, seesawed, and waltzed again. A few moments later Charlie reached down, planted this thumb in the fish's mouth, and lifted it.

"We both know this fellow," he said, showing me the pronounced blotches along the fish's lateral line and the little patch of teeth on the tongue. It was a Kentucky spotted bass.

I shot a picture or two, and Charlie released the bass to fight another day. Then one of the boys in the other boat whooped. We looked up to see a water explosion and Chet's little featherweight spinning rod bending almost double. Then the line parted.

"Ah, well," Chet called, "either my drag was too tight or I haven't got enough rod."

In the next mile we picked up several small bass. Then, at Don's suggestion, we cranked up our motors and headed downstream to the mouth of Silver Creek.

In olden days the Pearl River served as a waterway for settlers. Steamboats plied the river as far upstream as Edinburg in Leake County. As late as 1900 the U.S. Corps of Engineers' snagboat **Pearl** operated as far north as Rockport. A vast harvest of virgin logs was floated down the Pearl to sawmills in southern Mississippi. With the coming of the railroads, the river traffic ceased, and the Pearl settled back into the quiet pattern of a wilderness river.

The river widens about the mouth of Silver Creek, where there is a stretch of shallow bars. Loaded as we were, there was barely enough water to float our craft. When we caught up with the other boat, Don motioned for us to fish the mouth of the creek.

All around us was excellent bass water. One very promising spot was where the channels of the creek and river met. Our motor's lower unit grounded on a bar and brought us to a halt in a good position for casting.

"If we can sit here long enough," Charlie said, "I'll try topwater fishing."

He snapped on a surface lure with blades at each end. We made simultaneous casts, he to an eddy and I across the creek channel to shallow water over a submerged sand spit. I brought my underwater plug across the bar, and as it came off into deeper water a bass flashed out of the depths and nailed the lure solidly. Just as I set the hook, the surface splashed, and I saw that my partner had a bass, too. Both fish performed as though they were in a chorus line, kicking high most of the time since they couldn't bore deep in the shallow water.

"These spotted bass act like trout," Charlie observed after we'd brought the fish in. We agreed that the cool water of the river and the fact that the fish spend much of their lives fighting strong currents may enhance their acrobatic ability. Most of the fish weighed from 1 to 2 $\frac{1}{2}$ pounds, and light tackle was just right for them. We were told that some of those river bass weigh four pounds, but they're rare.

We caught several more bass in the mouth of Silver Creek and released all but two. We spent the remainder of the morning leap-frogging with the other boat to one good stretch of water after another. The Kentucky spotted bass (known locally as redeye bass) seemed to prefer eddies where the river narrows to sweep between a sandbar and a deep cutbank. We found such spots at almost every bend and concentrated on them. Fast water swirling around snags and drowned treetops were sure bets, too. If a stretch looked especially promising, we'd start the motor, run back upstream, and fish it again.

We caught up with the other boat well past noon, when the three other fishermen were working over the bassiest banks we'd seen all morning. Chet and Bob took a largemouth apiece out of the same treetop while Don held the boat in position with a paddle.

A short distance farther downstream, we nosed into the bank for lunch. While we ate, Don told us about an oxbow lake a few hundred yards back in the woods. There are many such lakes along the river, but this one was surrounded by a big hardwood swamp that was a paradise for game. We had to see it.

We couldn't put down a foot near the lake without stepping on deer tracks, and then we found fresh turkey scratchings. Charlie plucked a greenbriar leaf and made the notes of a turkey hen by blowing on it. I think we were both surprised when the three-note yelp of a turkey came from a ridgetop on our right. We grinned at one another, and Charlie whispered, "I'd sure like to be here come April."

That section of the Pearl seemed to be an Eden for game. We found alligator slides where the reptiles entered the river.

We fished only the best holes and put several bass into our ice chest for that fish fry that my wife Peg had promised us. Of all the lures we tried, spinners seemed most effective.

The sun was inching into the timber when we finally pulled up on a sandbar to meet Johnny, Don's tall 14-year-old son. He had a burlap sack full of mussels.

"Catfish bait for trotlines," Don explained. "I live only a few miles from here and asked the boy to gather these for us."

Johnny brought in a bucket from his narrow aluminum boat.

"If you fellas will help open a few of these," he said, "we'll soon have enough bait, and it's some of the best."

Chet picked up a mussel and knicked the edge of the shell to break the suction. Then he inserted the point of his knife and deftly twisted the mussel open, as he has done with many a clam in his native state. With everyone working at the job, the bucket was soon half filled with bait.

We camped on the next wide, white sandbar. With the tent up and a fire going, Chet and Charlie started supper while Bob, Don, and I baited 100 hooks with the mussels and set out the trotline. When we returned to camp half an hour later, potatoes were baking in the campfire coals, and five steaks were beginning to sizzle on the grill.

Chet had walked to the far end of the bar for a last try at the bass before dark, and I joined him.

It was that quiet time of day. The fading light brushed the Pearl with gold, except where a single snag protruded through the glass surface, and the current streamed past in twisting shades of silver. The campfire was beginning to make its own shadows, and I knew of no other place in the world I'd rather have been at that moment.

"We'd better run that trotline while we're still awake," Don suggested after supper. Bob and I agreed to help him while Chet and Charlie washed the supper dishes.

When we approached the snag to which we had tied the line, it was dipping and bobbing with the steady pulls of fish. On that first run we collected four good channel cats and a "motley"—a species of mudcat that is splotched with green and brown.

While we were rebaiting the hooks, Don casually reached out and picked up a water snake. Though it was a harmless variety, I was fascinated—as I am by all folks who handle snakes.

"Were you ever bitten?" Bob asked.

"I've got snakebite scars all over my hands," Don replied. "When I worked on a snake farm I was bitten by a fer-de-lance, which as you know is one of the world's most deadly reptiles. They wanted to lop off my finger with a meat cleaver right after it happened, but I wouldn't agree. I was in the hospital for weeks and lost over fifty pounds, but somehow I pulled through."

When we returned to camp with our catfish, we were greeted by a sonorous melody from the tent, and it didn't take us long to join the snorers' chorus.

I awoke to the cawing of a crow and found our tent evacuated. I threw back the flap and saw Charlie and Chet fishing near the end of the bar. I fired up the stove, put the coffee pot on, and then washed my face in the river's cool, clear water.

By the time the coffee had perked and the bacon was done, Bob and Don came roaring around the bend above camp with seven more catfish from our trotline. We polished off the bacon and eggs, and while the rest of us struck camp and loaded our gear, Don skinned the cats with a pair of dull nipper pliers that helped him to strip the skin as though peeling a ripe peach. We were on our way before the sun had cleared the trees.

That day Chet, Don, and I shared one boat while Bob and Charlie brought up the rear in the African Queen, our name for the heavily loaded supply craft.

It was another perfect morning on the river, with the singing current and a pleasant breeze. We had learned some of the tricks of river fishing the day before, and now we put them to good use. Don had fished the river since he was knee-high to a channel cat, and he knew where every bass was supposed to live. We put back a great many more bass than we kept.

Along about noon the breeze freshened, thunder rolled, and then streaks of lightning blasted both banks of the river. Before Chet, Don, and I could locate the African Queen, which carried all our raingear, we were hit by an old- fashioned chunk-floater that forced us to the bank.

The storm was over when we met Charlie and Bob on a sandbar for lunch. We were eating our sandwiches when we heard the hum of an outboard motor around the bend. Don pushed his boat into the river.

"Be right back," he said. "I'd better check to make sure they're legal."

The strangers turned out to be licensed fishermen—the only other anglers we saw during our two days on the Pearl.

As we drifted along after lunch—casting to cypress knees, stumps, snags, and treetops—Chet and I questioned Don about the river.

"Best bass and bream fishing is during spring and early summer," he told us. "Fishing is also good in October and November. The catfish hit best during high water in the early spring."

Presently the river is under development by a state agency called the Pearl River Basin Development District. Plans call for a channel-clearing program to open up navigation, giving inland communities an outlet to the sea. Reclamation of flooded areas and hydroelectric-power installations are planned, as is controlled water flow through the use of storage pools and a system of dams.

In addition, plans call for pollution abatement, boatways for big pleasure craft, and easy access via paved launching ramps. Channel-clearing in the lower Pearl and construction of sophisticated water parks and improved campsites are already under way.

Chet asked Don what he thought about the plans for the river. He pushed his cap back thoughtfully and said, "Well, it means lots of changes. It all depends on what you want the river to be."

Civilization makes changes, and we call these changes progress. The Pearl, as Donald Spence and his father have known it, is flowing along on borrowed time. True, it will soon be easier to navigate and will be more accessible to more people, but I'm glad we saw it while it was still a wilderness stream.

It was late afternoon when we rounded a bend and spotted Don's truck and boat trailer on the bank. Our trip was over. It didn't take us long to unload our gear and haul the boats. We were ready to leave when Chet asked a question:

"Don, this is a beautiful stretch of river. What lies beyond that next bend?"

It is the eternal question of the river voyageur. Maybe someday we'll find out. I sure hope so.

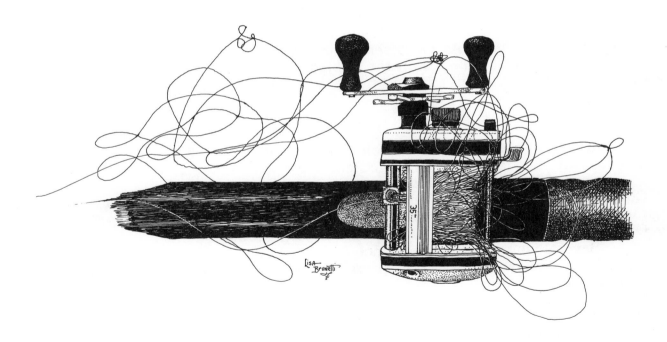

TONY McCLEB'S SECRET

Gene Nunnery

*Gene Nunnery, Meridian, is a businessman, inventor, outdoorsman, and amateur archaeologist. As an expert wild turkey hunter, Gene has penned one of the best-selling books on the subject—*The Old Pro Turkey Hunter, *and a second book* I Will Lift Up Mine Eyes Unto the Hills.

Along about this time, Gabe took a hankering to go down to Lane County and talk with Tony McCleb. I got the impression that Mr. Tony wasn't doing too good health-wise. Someone from Lane County gave a message to Gabe that Mr. Tony McCleb wanted to have a talk with him. Out of the great respect Gabe had for Tony, we took off in Gabe's old pickup truck for the domain of Tony McCleb.

Several years had passed since I had seen Mr. Tony. Matter of fact, the last time I saw him was the spring I killed that famous Lane County turkey, Gallberry Joe. That was five years ago, which would make Tony McCleb ninety-five years old. Gabe and I camped the same place we camped when hunting Gallberry Joe. The familiar surroundings brought back the memories of that eventful trip.

144

When we arrived at Tony McCleb's house, it did my heart good to see how glad Tony was to see us. Country folks get lonesome at times, and good company didn't come by every day or every week, for that matter. Gabe said to Tony, "Mr. Tony, the boy and me are going to be down this way for several days. If it is all right with you, we'll come over every morning we are here to visit with you." Mr. Tony, of course, agreed with that and came quickly to the point of telling Gabe why he had sent word that he wanted to see him. Tony said he realized his life was winding down and it was his hope that he could have one good long visit with Gabe before the end came. "I want to do some turkey talking with you, Gabe Meadow," said Tony.

I could tell that Tony McCleb had aged some. However, for his age, he was still a remarkable man. He and Gabe talked for about three hours each morning and I listened. If I could have recorded this last series of talks between Gabe Meadow and Tony McCleb, that recording would be my most prized possession. Tony may have slipped physically but certainly not mentally. Like a master host, he would frequently beam a tale in my direction. We were sitting on the porch one day when two of the many roosters on the place squared off for a fight. We all watched with interest and it reminded Tony of one of his childhood pranks. Tony said once he had a neighbor boy come over to spend a few days with him. The visiting boy was amazed at the number of roosters on the McCleb place and by the fact they hardly ever fought each other. Tony explained that the roosters had a pecking order—each knew the roosters who could whip him and the roosters he could whip. Tony said he had often figured on how to change the pecking order and start these roosters fighting. One day he figured a way but had not had a chance to try it. Perhaps now would be a good time. The whole McCleb chicken flock was a colorful sight. Every size and color you can imagine. Lots of white, red, black, yellow, and mixed colors. Tony and his boy guest slipped some corn out of the crib, some soot from the chimney, and some flour from the barrel in the pantry. With the corn, they caught every white and black rooster on the place. The black ones they covered with flour and the white ones they covered with soot. Tony said every rooster on the place became involved in a free-for-all. Roosters fought for three days. Tony said after about one day, his mama and papa joined the fight, having found out about Tony's prank. Tony said his ma and pa used up three plum bushes of switches on him and his friend. For the benefit of the "now" generation, it was customary in Tony's day for the host parents to discipline any "youngun" who might be under their roof.

The time had come for Gabe and me to go home. Gabe told Tony at the beginning of the last morning session we would be leaving that day.

When Gabe announced that we were going home, a kind of eerie silence fell on our group. For a short time nothing was said, and that was unusual around Tony McCleb. In a few minutes, Tony arose slowly from his huge rocking chair and said, "Let's take a walk down the road a piece." Gabe and I followed as Tony carefully and slowly led us down the narrow road to a point overlooking the entire valley of the beautiful Buckatuna River. There by the road stood one of the largest white oak trees I ever saw. Tony sat down and leaned against this huge tree and indicated for Gabe and me to do the same. From our vantage point, the green valley of the Buckatuna River wound its way southward. The valley was completely covered with timber—hardwood along the river, pine on the gentle slopes leading to the ridges. Tony said, "This here oak was here when I was a boy. Course t'was smaller then. I have leaned against it all these years, physically and mentally. When I get tired physically, I come here and sit and it rests me. When my mind is disturbed or I need to do some thinking, I come and sit and my mind soon gets settled. The peace of the valley seems to come up here better than any other place I know." After a few more minutes of small talk, Tony's mood changed to one of austere seriousness.

"Gabe," Tony said, "I have known you for many, many years. You are the most dedicated wild turkey man I ever knew. The fact that you have taken this boy [me] under your wing, speaks well of him. I have decided to share a secret with you two which has been closely guarded by the McCleb clan for generations and generations. More than eight generations have passed it down. As you know, me and my cousins, Deak and Zeke, are the last of the McClebs. I don't have any boys to pass the secret to. It wouldn't do to turn the secret over to Deak and Zeke, that's for sure. Now y'all just settle back and listen careful to what I am going to tell you." You could tell that Tony had wrestled with this decision-making for some time and now that he had resolved it, he was at peace.

Tony McCleb's eyes sparkled with enthusiasm as he began to lay out this remarkable story. He said, "I don't have to tell you what an outlandish creature a wild turkey really is. In all this world there is no creature that comes close to being what a wild turkey is. Because a wild turkey is so different, it takes a special breed of men to deal with him and to appreciate him. Then out of this special breed of men, a few rise above the rest to become what I call 'turkey men.' Now you turkey men listen to this."

Tony laid it out with quiet, convincing tones. "The most curious creature on this earth is a monkey. The next most curious is a wild turkey. Remember that. If a turkey sees a man, he leaves in a hurry. If a turkey sees or hears a dog, he does the same. He instantly recognizes by sight and sound all of his enemies. The fox or the bobcat will half scare him out of his wits and he quickly runs or flies from them. But if a wild turkey sees something he has never seen before, his overpowering curiosity gets a hold of him, simply paralyzes him with the desire to find out what the unfamiliar thing is. He will hold his ground as this new thing approaches, hoping to find out what it is. Only a turkey man is going to believe what I am now going to tell y'all. You run into this old turkey who won't come to you, and everything else in your bag of tricks fails. Others as well as you have failed to kill him and it seems he is not to be had. He may be invincible to all others, but not to the men who possess the McCleb secret. This old turkey is out there and you are going to get him. Here is how. After you locate him, stop right there and start taking off your clothes. Take off every stitch, even your hat, your shoes, and socks. Get just as naked as the day you came into this world. Now get down on your all fours—that is, your hands and knees—and start backing toward the turkey. If you do it right, the turkey will be so paralyzed with curiosity at the sight you present to him, he just ain't going to run or fly. He's got to find out what it is. He may walk around in small circles clucking, but he ain't going nowhere. Boys, take my word for it. This trick works. McClebs have used it for generations and it helped earn for all of them great reputations. I have used it. Now guard it careful and use it only when you have to."

When Tony McCleb finished this episode, he sat back with eyes closed. Seems like he wanted us to take the time to let his secret soak in. I have never seen Gabe in quite the state of confusion he was in now. He didn't know what to say. Whether to thank Tony or not; whether to accept this secret as a gift or as an amusing anecdote. Of course, it completely flabbergasted me.

The talk turned to other subjects as we made our way back to Tony's house. Never once did Tony mention the secret again. When we got ready to go, Tony thanked us for our visits and talks.

Would you believe that to this day, Gabe Meadow has never mentioned the Tony McCleb secret. Mr. Tony said the monkey holds first place as the most curious creature. In second place is the wild turkey. At that time, in third place went Gene Nunnery. I earned that place due to the great degree of curiosity I had to find out what Gabe thought about Tony's secret. I have had to live over forty years with this secret gnawing at my curiosity. If Gabe had just given me his opinion, it would have eased my mind. Foxy old Tony McCleb knew how to be remembered. His love for entertaining goes on even after his life has passed.

Was this Tony McCleb secret one big joke? Was it, in fact, a true and normal tactic that would work on a turkey? I have pondered these facts and am now just as uncertain about the entire matter as I was the day Tony McCleb stunned Gabe and me with it. I know for a fact that wild turkeys have great curiosities. I know, also, that their reaction to any situation is most unpredictable. As I have said before, I will believe almost anything a person tells me about a wild turkey. On several occasions, I have been tempted to try the Tony McCleb secret. I may try it yet. Anyway, I feel a lot better about it, since sharing this secret with you. It helps some to have others ponder this turkey tale for what it is worth.

Lisa Brunetti   **149**

A SORT OF CONFESSION

Jim Ritchie

Murder is a dark and ugly word. It sounds even more repugnant when you may be guilty of it, which I may be. I don't know whether it was actually murder or not. Sometimes I think it was, and sometimes I don't. You can be the judge of that. I was never prosecuted by the law for it. I'm sometimes prosecuted by my conscience.

I killed a friend of mine. With a rifle, and with what the law calls "malice aforethought," even though the period of "aforethought" was only about five minutes. It was not done in a period of anger, nor in a period of temporary insanity, nor was it accidental, nor was it because of righteous jealousy, nor done in self-defense. I simply pointed a rifle between his eyes and pulled the trigger. And he died instantly. His name was Tom. His registered, legal name was Frierson's Tom Boy. He was an orange and white English Pointer. He wasn't the very best bird dog I ever owned, but in the important things, he was the most special. He was hardheaded, bad to fight, almost unpennable, and a semi-outlaw. And he loved me. And I loved him. I still do.

I first met Sir Tom on the heels of another tragedy. I had just lost the best bird dog I'd ever hunted behind. I mean he was perfect. I had trained him myself from his puppyhood. He could find quail like he used radar, he was staunch on point, he honored other dogs on point as far as he could see them, he was like a vacuum cleaner finding dead birds, and he retrieved to hand without mussing a feather. His name was Rip, and he was a gentleman. I almost never had to even raise my voice to him. I simply turned him loose and let him perform.

When I lost Rip, I immediately started looking for another dog. I decided this time to buy a trained dog and settled temporarily on probably the most beautiful pointer I'd ever seen. His name was Beau, and he absolutely drew stares wherever we went. He was gorgeous. A classic lemon and white pointer whose style on point would make the hair on the back of your neck stand up. Problem was that the sound of a shot would cause him to flinch. He wouldn't flinch bad, but he would flinch enough for me to suspect that he was a little soft.

Pete Frierson told me when I bought him to bring him back if I had any problem with him. So I took him back to Pete and explained the problem. I told him that I would really prefer to have a dog who was a little bolder. Pete said, "Son, if bold is what you're after, I think you'll like this one." That's when I met Sir Thomas.

Pete's trainer, Fred Bridges, walked me over to Tom's pen and introduced us. "Jim," Fred drawled, "you know I'll shoot straight with you. This is a good dog. He's got a good nose and he knows what to do. But in my forty years of training dogs, I can honestly say that this is the hard-headedest, cantankerdest, orneriest dog I have ever handled. He can climb out of Alcatraz, he'll fight another dog in a New York minute, and he'll try your patience in every way a dog can try a man until you convince him that you're his boss. You're going to have to put your bull in his pasture and not let him get away with the least little thing until you convince him that you're serious about what you tell him to do. But once you remove his doubts, I think you'll be pleased with him. If you aren't, bring him back and we'll keep trying 'till we find one that suits you."

I looked at the three-year-old dog, and he looked at me. I got the distinct feeling that we were actually appraising each other. He was about average size for a pointer, but he was wide-chested and had a pretty heavy coat of muscle. I figured he weighed about sixty pounds. His head was wide, leaving plenty of room for brains between those amber eyes, which met my gaze in a straightforward look that left no doubt in my mind that he was alert, bright, and confident. His tail was up and wagging in short, muscular whips. His muzzle was a little too short for him to be a really good looking dog, and his big mouth was open with a long tongue hanging out one corner in a kind of lopsided, tongue-lolling grin. I didn't even look at another dog. As he loaded into my car, Fred, after telling me the commands he used with Tom, reminded me, a little differently this time, "Remember, Jim, if you don't like him, or *can't handle him*, bring him back."

I never took him back, but I did consider it a few times in the beginning. I found out on our first hunting trip that Fred had described Tom to a "T". The frustrating part of dealing with him was that he knew what I wanted him to do, but was enough of a delinquent to just challenge me either by not paying a bit of attention to my commands, or worse, pausing to let me know that he heard and understood, then proceeding to do whatever the hell he wanted to do. Which was almost never what I wanted him to do.

Now, I don't like corporal punishment. I didn't like to get it, and I never liked to give it—to my kids or to my dogs. And I always used it as the absolutely last resort. But with Tom, I figured there was no other way, and the trainer's advice seemed more and more to acquire validity. Except in Tom's case, corporal punishment wasn't enough. After a good switching with a whippy hickory, he'd grin as if to say "Thanks, Boss," and go his merry way again. Corporal punishment escalated to sergeant punishment, then to captain, then to colonel. The first three times I took him out, I shot him a total of five times.

I'd command "Come here;" he'd pause, look at me, and head in the other direction. When I was sure that the eyes and vital parts weren't exposed, and when enough distance was between us, I'd burn his fanny with number 8s and he would turn and come to me. Finally, after the fifth shot on the third trip, I guess he decided that when I said "Come here," I meant *Come Here*, and we never had that problem again. Once we settled that little misunderstanding and I was able to call him to me, I had to add another item of equipment to my arsenal.

It was a piece of rubber hose about two feet long. I'm talking about the reinforced kind that you hook up washing machines with. The regular rubber hoses didn't last long with Tom.

Now, before you get all stirred up about what a cruel S.O.B. I am who would shoot a poor dog with birdshot and tear his rear up with a rubber hose, and before you pick up that phone to call the Society for the Prevention of Cruelty to Animals, you need to understand that I was dealing with a special case here. Tom was... well, he was...physical. That's what he was. Physical. He'd point, then run the birds up, come to me when I called him, cheerfully take his whipping, and head out again. I think he was sort of Presbyterian because he always seemed glad to get that predestined event over and go on to the next situation. He never pouted or became cowed, even when I really got tough with him.

One time Bill Cook and I were hunting with Tom and my other dog, Sue, and it had been a long, unproductive day. The quail had just seemed to evaporate from the face of the earth. We hadn't located a single one all day. Finally, in the afternoon, old Susie pointed right up on the top of a bald hill in short grass. Tom rounded the crest of the hill, saw her pointed, and skidded to a perfect honoring point like a gentleman should, about ten yards behind her. Bill and I kicked into high gear to get up there and flush the birds. It was going to be an ideal situation where a wide-open shot was inevitable, and we were both thinking of a double or triple each. At last, some excitement!

Tom sort of got excited too, I guess. Just before we got into gun range, for reasons known only to him, he shot past Susie and ran those birds up. Must have been about thirty of them fanning out in a storybook covey rise. Then the culprit decided to *chase* a low-flying bird which

153

fortunately, led him right by me. I tackled him, grabbed his collar, took a half turn in the collar so he couldn't pull out, put a foot on his hindquarters, and went to work on him with the hose, hollering "Whoa" with every lick.

Well, I whipped him until I thought I was going to have a heart attack. When I finally quit, he didn't get up. I hadn't realized that when I took the turn in his collar, I had cut off his wind. He was sort of unconscious. I reached down and pumped on his ribs a few times and he got up and staggered around for a minute. Then he looked at me as if to say, "O.K., I think I understand. Now, which way did those birds go?" In less than five minutes he was frozen on a single point, and he honored Susie's point several times later that afternoon. That day was the last time he failed to honor a point. I even found him pointed in the woods once honoring an old refrigerator somebody had dumped. I guess he figured the white thing might be another dog, and he wasn't close enough to see that it wasn't. And maybe he was remembering....

All of the situations weren't exasperating. After a while, the trips began to take on more of a bird-hunting flavor instead of arm-thrashing exercise sessions, and the diminishing number of violations sometimes even added a little humor.

He was stuck on a single bird one afternoon, pointing solid as a rock. He had the bird dead to rights and I was on my way to him when I saw the danger signal flash. His tail, normally rigid at about a sixty-degree angle, was moving slightly side-to-side. This meant one of three things: A. He wasn't sure he had the bird located; B. He wasn't sure what it was he was pointing; or C. More likely than A or B, he was going to flush the bird himself. This particular time, he performed C. The quail went whirring off, I called him to me, and he and I and the rubber hose had our regular meeting. After the meeting, he disappeared over the hill in front of us which was, in fact, just where I wanted him to go. When I reached the top of the hill, there was Tom, rock-solid pointed again in a patch of broomsedge. And his tail started moving again. I admit to having had a sinking feeling because I was worn out from our last little tete-a-tete, and I wasn't sure I could perform effectively again that quickly. So I hollered "Whoa", just to let him know I was watching. I knew that his fanny had to still be burning. At the sound of my voice, four deer jumped up from their beds in the broomsedge ahead of Tom and took off lickety-split. Tom didn't move. Then he slowly turned his head and looked at me and said without speaking, "Look, *you* ran them up. I didn't even know what they were. But I figured I'd better wait 'til you got here. So leave that hose in your hunting sack." I grinned and sent him on.

Lord, how he loved to fight! He was a perfect gentleman as long as he was around a female dog, but with the slightest provocation from another male, Tom would be on him like white on rice, and he'd hang with it 'til times got better. Or until I'd somehow break it up.

I've always kept my bird dogs penned. (In Tom's case, the pen floor was concrete and the pen had to have a completely wired top.) The neighborhood we lived in at this particular time was occupied by a big German Shepherd who ran loose and was the scourge of the other canine neighborhood occupants. He was a bully who had whipped every unpenned dog in the area. There was no question as to who was king of that hill.

One afternoon I turned Tom and Sue loose for an exercise run in a large field nearby and I was following a leisurely couple of hundred yards behind them, just keeping them in sight. I saw that big shepherd come sailing out of some high grass and make a snapping pass at Susie. Tom was on him in a heartbeat. By the time I ran to them, blood was flying in all directions and a sure-enough serious dogfight was in progress. I sort of dived in the middle of it and somehow got them apart, swooped up the bloody Tom in my arms, and ran home to survey the damage. I gingerly began to wash off the blood, dreading what I might find. The more I washed, the more puzzled I became. None of the blood was his. There wasn't a nick on him. I couldn't believe he had given away twenty pounds to a heavyweight German Shepherd and had come out unquestionably on top. But he had. He turned his head and looked at me with that lopsided, tongue-lolling grin, and I'll swear he was trying to tell me, "That was fun! I enjoyed the fight and the bath, but Boss, I especially enjoyed the ride home!" And the shepherd gave our house a wide berth after that day.

Like I said earlier, Tom was physical. He liked for me to put my hands on him or to just touch him in some way. When I'd turn him out of his pen, he'd dance around me and grin and bounce like most dogs do, but he wouldn't jump up on me because he knew I didn't allow that. Still he had to touch somehow, so he'd dance around behind me and *nibble* at the seat of my pants. No bites, or even nips. More like bounce and nibble and bounce and nibble. Anything for friendly contact.

His downfall started one day when he and I were hunting alone on our farm. He had pointed a covey of birds and was standing in a patch of knee-high honeysuckle. He wasn't broken to wing and shot, so when I kicked the birds up, he jumped as he always did. I didn't see exactly what happened, but one of the honeysuckle vines evidently tripped him up. In any event, he landed in some freak way so that he shattered his right shoulder. I heard one little yelp of pain. No loud screaming or crying, though the pain must have been fierce. Just that one little yelp. My truck was parked at the house three-quarters of a mile away. I bedded him down in the honeysuckle and raced to the truck so I could pick him up and rush him to the vet. I bumped over that pasture in the pickup like there was no tomorrow, and when I got to where I'd left him, he wasn't there. A frantic search followed and I finally found him about halfway home. He had an absolutely shattered shoulder and had tried to quietly follow me home.

156

After the trip to the vet's office, the x-rays, the cast, the pills, etc., I took him home, but irreparable damage had been done. For several weeks he'd try to walk, but the cast was too long and bulky to allow it, so the best he could do was a sort of dragging shuffle, and he began to weaken. After a couple of subsequent trips to the vet, I was advised that I should leave him there to be put down.

I had to think about that for a while, so I took him home that final time. He was nine years old, and the old recuperating ability just wasn't there. I resigned myself after two days of thinking about it that the vet's suggestion would be the best course, so the next morning I went to his pen to get him and carry him on his last journey.

He was lying on his belly, too weak to move anything but his head and tail. I picked him up and carried him out of the pen to a shady spot where we could talk. And I talked, and he listened for a change. It was then that I decided on a slightly different course. We had walked too many miles together, shared too many triumphs together, and loved each other too much for me to allow him to die under the hands of a relative stranger in the one confusing, antiseptic place he hated. So I got up, went into the house and got my rifle, loaded it, and killed him.

I wrapped him in a good bedsheet from the house, placed him in the pickup along with a shovel, and started our one-vehicle procession to the north forty for the burial. I picked out a gravesite in a grove of oaks where he had found his last covey of birds before the accident, and started to dig.

I don't cry much. Real men don't do that, I'm given to understand. But that day I exited the ranks of real men for the first time in twenty years. I'd forgotten that the first tears burn as badly as sweat in the eyes and that a contraction begins deep down in the groin and that involuntary spasmodic jerks move up the abdomen to the gut and the chest and strangled noises percolate up through all that to a tight throat and blast out loud enough to be heard for a quarter of a mile. I'd forgotten that mucus and saliva mix into strings tough enough so that when you try to spit, the strings won't turn loose and have to be semi-smeared on a shoulder or a sleeve. I'd forgotten that during the course of all this carrying on, it helps to be able to *attack* something like tough goddam oak roots with a goddam dull shovel in hard, dry goddam dirt so that the main attention can be turned to the difficult physical task at hand and slow the goddam crying. That works for a few minutes until the corner of the eye accidentally catches a glimpse of a bloody sheet, and the whole goddam process starts all over again.

The burial took hours. Then, when I'd dried out inside and outside, I drove back to the house and smilingly told the family that I'd buried old Tom in a good place.

That occurred years ago. Time, of course, has dimmed the event some, but I still remember one small segment as if it had happened this morning. Just before I pulled the trigger, he looked me straight in the eye, grinned that lopsided grin, and scraped his tail across the ground in a feeble wag. I think he was trying to tell me he understood. I hope I was right. I hope he understood.

Please, God, I hope he understood.

THE NIGHT BEFORE

Joe L. McDonald

Joe L. McDonald, Williamsburg, is the former owner and editor of the Stone County Enterprise *weekly newspaper at Wiggins and has worked as editor and writer for several other newspapers. He is currently District Public Information Officer for the Mississippi Forestry Commission, and editor of the agency's* Forestry Forum *magazine. He is Outdoors Editor for the* Brookhaven Daily Leader *and writes a syndicated general interest column. Joe is a regular free-lance contributor to magazines and newspapers as well as an after-dinner humorist.*

It is the night before opening morning of deer season, and I'm in my kitchen rocking chair getting my gear ready for leaving at pre-dawn. The teapot clock whistles the time is eight o'clock.

"Hey, you're pointing that thing toward me—it isn't loaded, is it?" my wife says and asks in a single utterance.

"Of course it is. I always clean a loaded double barreled shotgun in the kitchen. See, I'm looking down the barrels now to see if there's any dirt," I say jokingly. Only, she doesn't hear the comment as a joke and doesn't return the smile I flashed when I said it. Instead, she studies intently the spaghetti sauce she is stirring.

She apparently is in no joking mood, so proceed cautiously, I warn myself. One spurious comment could end my hunt 10 hours before it begins. And keep in mind, too, that the 10 chores she assigned me two months ago still are uncompleted.

"No, seriously, the gun isn't loaded, and I apologize for pointing it your way. Any idiot should know better. Unloaded guns kill people. It won't happen again, I promise," I answer, being serious in mood as I say it.

"Why do you have to clean it, anyway? You haven't fired it at a deer the past ten years."

That was a low blow. But it's okay, I console myself, she's only teasing, trying to provoke me into making an irrational comment that she could later use against me. I must remain cool, must not bite a baited trap.

"Guns need cleaning, whether they've been fired or not. Dirt-dobbers sometimes build nests in the barrels of guns stored in closets. My uncle once fired a gun with a dirt-dobber nest in the barrel and the shot ripped out the side as if the barrel was made of paper. Not only can dirt-dobbers be a problem, but lint and dust collect in barrels and can affect the gun's shooting accuracy. One ball of lint no larger than a tiny wart can cause a bullet fired from 20 yards away to miss its target by 18.5 feet. As a matter of incidental information, you calculate that by dividing the size of the wart-like obstruction in the barrel by the distance from the target and multiply by pi." (I figure the equation will convince her I know what I'm talking about.)

"Maybe so. But you don't really think you'll get a shot at a deer tomorrow?" she asks.

"You can bet on it. Buck McCousins has already staked out a big 10-point. He's been checking the deer's scrapes and tracks for two weeks, and its pattern is well established—and documented, up here," I say, pointing to my brain. "This is gonna be my year—you just have the freezer contents arranged to accommodate the meat I'll bring home tomorrow night."

"I'll just wait until you return before I move anything in the freezer," she comments, steadily stirring the spaghetti sauce.

What is this? Hey, lady, Miss Know-It-All Person, what is this—roast your husband tonight? Give me a break here, Motor Mouth Queen. I know how to shoot a gun. I know deer hunting. I might not be a lucky person, but everybody's luck has to change sometimes. That's what I want to say, but I actually say, "As you wish."

Placing my boots beside the rocking chair, I set two boxes of shotgun shells on the kitchen table, hang my cap on a door knob, wrap my heavy coat round the chair-back, and begin sacking grub for the hunt.

"If I can help you find something, please ask now, because I don't want you waking me at 4 a.m. to ask," she remarks.

"Never mind. I've got everything together I'll need. I will ease out of bed and be long gone before you awake."

"You're absolutely certain now—you don't need my help finding anything?"

"Certain. But you could show me where the onions are. Gotta have an onion with sardines."

She criticizes the sardines because she doesn't eat them, but I explain that a deer hunt is never completely satisfying unless the hunter eats sardines at lunch. I demonstrate, by pantomime, how one licks up the packing oil that spills from the can and oozes down the arms as the tiny fish are eaten without the aid of fork or paper towels. She doesn't smile at the pantomime.

I drag out from a cabinet shelf a first-aid kit and check its contents. The kit needs aspirin, but I'm not sure where she has placed them, and I dare not ask.

"Expecting to be wounded?"

"No, but you never know when you might cut a finger on a sardine can. Have I told you about the time Buck and I were up in..."

"You told me, you told me. Now, are you sure you have everything?"

161

I assure her that I do, and soon I'm listening to the television weatherman predicting low temperatures, high winds, and rain mixed with sleet for tomorrow. Ideal weather conditions for opening day of deer season.

Later, in bed, I toss and turn as I anticipate the hunt that now is only a few hours away. Sleep eludes me; I check the clock; get up and smoke a cigarette; go back to bed and toss and turn.

Next morning, in my kitchen rocking chair, I lace my boots, lashing the strings tightly round the top portion above my ankles, the way foresters tie their boots to prevent dangling strings that might cause you to trip.

I load up my gear in the car. But my orange vest is missing. It must be in the hallway closet. I walk softly down the hallway so as not to wake her.

Inside the closet I can see many things, but I don't see the orange vest. It must be behind the books on the top shelf. I will need a chair to stand in to look behind the books.

The chair, carefully brought down the hallway from the kitchen, bumps the closet door as I position it for standing on. Pausing momentarily, I listen but hear no stirring sounds in the bedroom where she is sleeping. So I proceed, climbing onto the chair. As I reach up, the chair moves and I tumble, pulling books on top of me. I worry more about the noise than injury. Still, the bedroom is silent.

The vest is not behind the books after all. I find it hanging among the coats as it should be. I then tip-toe up the hallway, exit through the kitchen, and climb back into my car. Did I switch off the coffee pot?

Back in the kitchen checking the coffee pot, that wise voice inside my head tells me to check my wallet for my hunting license. I am thankful for that voice because no license can be found in my wallet. Where is the darn thing?

162

I search the pockets of my coat in the car—nothing. It is in none of the kitchen drawers. Neither is it lying on any tables in the house. I even look in the cracker box I had taken crackers from while packing my grub sack. It is not in the refrigerator. What about the freezer? No, we decided to wait until I return from the hunt before moving items in the freezer to make room for the deer meat.

The bedroom door opens quietly, a streak of light from the hallway falls across her bed, but she does not move, does not speak. Clearing my throat, very softly, I speak in a whisper, "Do you hear me, sweetheart?"

"No, I do not hear you. I am still sleeping soundly. WHAT DO YOU WANT?"

"Remember the window cleaning you asked me to do, and that dirt you wanted me to spread, and the pine straw you begged me to sweep off the roof? I promise I'll do all those chores, along with all the others you've asked me to do the last six months, and anything else you can think of—I'll do them all day after tomorrow. I promise."

"You can't find your hunting license, can you?"

"No. I mean, yes, I can't. But I have everything else."

FLY-FISHING MISSISSIPPI SALT

Jim Slater

Jim Slater, Edwards, is a free-lance writer and outdoor photographer who covers big game tournaments from Mississippi to the British Virgins, and was selected as one of two American outdoor writers to attend the South African International Billfish Tournament. He is author of the forthcoming book, Salt On a Fly's Tail, *and is former co-host/producer of the award-winning outdoor television series,* Hawgs 'n Horns.

Expect the adrenaline rush to begin right at the end of the first full cast when the falling bait lightly breaks the water's surface and begins its gradual descent to a calculated depth. With line in hand, you have time to pull the sleek streamer only a couple of strokes forward before it's engulfed and ravaged by a 30-lb. set of toothy predatory choppers. The blacktip, realizing something's amiss, and with a remarkable show of force, explodes through the surface, soaring out of the water with a superb display of acrobatics. The hot reel drag hums as this fast and powerful gamefish makes its long dash out across the flats, taking line, backing, and 8-lb. leader to the limits. A sensational rush of bodily fluids becomes commonplace when the freshwater angler turns his fly rod seaward to ply the salt.

Saltwater fly fishing is probably a hundred years old by now. From canoes, class tarpon were being hooked on flies along the Florida coast during the early part of this century. As in freshwater angling, relatively few saltwater sportsmen choose to devote themselves to the purity and art of the fly rod. Only during the past several years has saltwater fly-rodding grown in popularity to the point of becoming a serious sport. Once a few heart-pounders have been hooked with a long thin stick and light drag reel, the bug has bitten! That old salt-spotted broomstick crankin' rig with its 50-lb. pink mono is destined for an attic dust treatment.

Many fresh and saltwater bait crankers are finding out that the pure heads-up excitement of playing a 30- or 40-lb. streak of lightning on a saltwater fly is a totally exhilarating experience. The tackle is lighter, the fish are bigger; the number of species, angling situations, and recreational opportunities available to the sportsfisherman are almost unlimited.

The Gulf Coast is wide open for the novice or "salty" fly-rodder to practice his art. Bays, lagoons, inlets, rivers, and all sorts of other coastal structure, both natural and artificial, abound with easy access to both shallow and deep water fisheries. The barrier islands off the mainland provide deep channels and passes along with highly productive lagoons, marshes, and skinnywater flats. Farther out, the Chandeleurs, production rigs, and open waters encourage some of the best fishing in the Gulf.

Let's think about equipment for a minute. It's easy to enter the world of saltwater flying. There are probably about as many favorite tackle variations as there are fly fishermen. But a few basics should at least be considered when putting a saltwater fly rig together.

Many species of gamefish found along the Gulf Coast can be caught with medium to heavy rods. Most flounder, speckled trout, and reds can be readily taken on a 5- to 8-weight rod loaded with matching line and the right leader. A lot of freshwater anglers already use a rod in one of these weight classes for trout, bass, bream, and other landlocked species. So, it's really no trouble to convert over to saltwater. The larger "bull" reds, cobia, dolphin, sharks, mackerel, and tarpon, however, can sometimes play havoc with this lighter equipment.

Fly rods in the 9-foot/9-weight class seem to have become the standard all-around caliber for most saltwater action. The length provides for enough casting height when wading chest deep or working from a low skiff or jon boat. This weight stick, loaded with a weight-forward tapered line and leader, provides great casting and distance control under windy conditions, and is tough enough to play and land a good 30 or 40 lb. lunker. For those bluewater freight trains, white marlin, sailfish, tarpon, and the like, a good quality rod from a 10- to 11-weight light tarpon rig to a 12- to 13-weight heavy-duty system would be appreciated.

A most important point to consider is matching the right reel to the right rod. Many good wall-hangers have been lost due to an initial break-off. While most of the playing on a fly rod is done with line in hand, a reel with a good positive drag system can spell success instead of "R-O-L-A-I- ...." A soft-touch drag that will smoothly release without sticking at the instant of strike will help prevent a 4-lb. class leader tippet from snapping. That same reel, when tightened up all the way, should be able to slow down that running bluefish and eventually hold him where you want him. However, a smooth drag with a soft low-end release is much more important than horsepower.

Fill the reel with the proper amount of 20-or 30-lb. Dacron backing before attaching the fly line. This can be from 150 to 250 yards of backing for most saltwater reels. It helps in preventing tight coils from forming in the line. And, should that bluefish decide to take a hundred-yard run, you can anchor that fighting butt in your belt and watch the show.

Now, we get to lines and leaders. Most people who are unfamiliar with fly-rodding automatically think of surface fishing with a tiny feathery fly or bug resting lightly on the water's surface and tied to the end of a floating line. True, surface casting and floating lines are important when fishing the salt. A weight-forward floating line with a short leader casts well in the wind and is much easier to pick up off the surface for the backward cast. Great in shallow water, a floating fly line combined with a 5- or 6-foot leader allows a weighted fly to hang a couple feet below the surface and a dry fly to ride high. When you're running the buoys and a 35-lb. cobia sucks the bristles right off of that deer hair surface popper, you've made your day! But a fly rod rigged with a sinking line and weighted bugs can take you to new depths.

The favorite sinking line of many is the Wet Cel Monocore, lovingly referred to as the "slime line" by a lot of anglers, with a modified weight-forward saltwater taper. Sinkers like this are good for use in tidal currents and to take that irresistible fly right down to where the money is.

Leaders are very important to fly presentation. Lengths may vary according to personal preference, wind conditions, the fish you're after, and the depth you want to go. A short 5- or 6-foot straight leader works well in a breeze and in murky water on both floating and wet lines. A longer tapered leader, some up to 15- or 20-foot on a floating line will allow a weighted bug to drop several feet below the surface. And, there's less chance of spooking some nervous bonefish in very shallow water.

Of some 800 species of fish found along the shore and in the open waters of the Gulf of Mexico, there are around 200 that sportfishermen are more likely to encounter one way or another. Distribution and habitat account for various species being favored for food and sport in one coastal area and not in another. Southern Florida boasts large populations of bonefish, permit, and tarpon, while other regions may prefer redfish and speckled trout simply because there are more of them!

There are three or four important species of inshore sportfish found in Gulf waters that seem to be favored by many anglers, though a large number of the other valued "200" should not be considered less. Spotted seatrout (speckled trout, or *Cynoscion nebulosus* if you want to get personal) can be found spawning near open water in sounds and bays from early to mid-spring right on through to early fall. The early evening is a good time to catch them in the act. Specks tend to spend much of their time around inshore areas and barrier shallows. Adult specks may retreat to a little deeper water after the spawn, but the young drift in and stay close to grassflats, salt marshes, and shallow areas close to shore. Since their natural habitat is relatively close in, they are considered a non-migratory species, and can be found in most coastal areas during most of the year, with the warm spring and summer period being the best time. The present IGFA world-record speck caught on a fly rod using a 16-lb. class tippet is 12-lb. 7-oz. The largest on record is 16-lb., which can probably be improved upon.

Specks are generally considered bottom dwellers, though they can be hooked at most any reasonable depth. They seem to have a taste for shrimp (a succulent pink or green shrimp fly might be in order here), but won't turn their nose up at a shiny fish (perhaps a long flashy streamer?).

The popular redfish, or red drum, holds a high place on the list of favorite table fare. As a sportfish, pound for pound, it's hard to beat. This tough fighter can run up to almost a hundred pounds, matching any degree of skill with a fly rod. Reds spawn in offshore shallows during the late summer and on into the fall season. Youngsters make their way to inshore habitats around pilings and breakwaters, while most of the larger adult reds, "bull" reds, like to hang out around deeper passes and channels. Reds prefer a diet of crabs and shrimp. Crab fly and grass shrimp variations would be good flies to consider. A streamer or two might add variety.

Southern flounder are easily found along mainland and island shores, around structure, and in quiet pools and estuaries during the warm months of the year. They are quick and strong, but the fight lasts only a short time. Wading around in the surf and casting into rocks, piers, and under docks can produce some exciting action and a great evening meal. Don't look for too many flounder during the winter months. When the

168

water gets cold, they move out into the deep. Some species have been seen by divers a hundred feet down on natural and artificial reefs, piled a couple of feet thick on top of each other. A good weighted variation of a shrimp fly swimming just off the bottom would work well on these flatfish.

Cobia (ling) can be a tough act to follow. The present IGFA saltwater fly rod record for 16-lb. class tippet is 83-lb. 4-oz. Cobia are drawn to large objects like buoys, production rigs, and even other larger fish. Generally, they will eat just about anything that comes along. So, any racy fly from a surface popper or ground mullet to a weighted streamer might do the trick. Cobia are very seasonal and will show up along the Gulf Coast toward the end of the third week in March.

Ship Island, Cat Island, and Horn Island, as well as the other barrier islands off Mississippi, are easily reached by boat. A craft with a little freeboard would sometimes be advisable, but the water is usually calm enough for an enjoyable ride out and back. The channel markers and buoy lines are favorite places to pause a while and throw a fly to surfacing cobia. The grassflats and shell reefs around the Chandeleurs are a bit farther out and offer some great speck and early fall red fishing. The mouth of the Pearl River and the Louisiana marshes have been known to hold some 200-pound-class tarpon that would stretch anyone's line.

According to the Marine Recreational Fisheries Statistics Survey, during one recent year's period, 689,000 speckled trout were caught on hook and line in Mississippi waters. That same year some 123,000 reds, 85,000 southern flounder, 163,000 Spanish Mackerel, and 40,000 sharks were reported hauled in by anglers. The fish are there! The vast aquatic resources along Mississippi's short frontage provide the fly-rodder with some of the most productive fishing grounds in the Gulf of Mexico.

Frances Drake

TIME OF DISTINCTION

Tony Kinton

Tony Kinton, Carthage, is a church musician as well as Mississippi Editor for Outdoor Life *magazine. He writes a syndicated newspaper column, and is a free-lance photographer and writer for magazines. Tony is author of three books—*The Beginning Bowhunter, Food For Game, *and the forthcoming* Outside and Other Reflections.

What it is about fall that makes it such a time of distinction is difficult to say. And to use a word no more powerful and picturesque than distinction to describe it is ludicrous; fall goes far beyond being merely distinct. That season is the champion, the winner of nature's beauty contest, a collection of days and nights that stands above and apart from the other collections of days and nights found in a year. Fall sparkles.

I suppose the things that make fall special to one may or may not be those that make it special to another. That is acceptable, even encouraged; one of the appealing attributes of autumn is the flexibility in sentimentality it affords. For me it is endearing for many reasons—some of which belong to the past, others more contemporary.

When I was a child cotton was a popular crop of every rural family. One acre, five acres, perhaps as many as twelve—most fields weren't large but they were surely present. Fall was the time to gather the fluffy fruit of this plant.

Cotton picking then was not what it was to become. No giant machines rumbled through the stalks—a dusty, lint-thick haze billowing from their basket cages then trailing behind. The labor was more genteel, quiet. Although some farms hosted an impressive array of hired hands at picking time, ours was much more modest. My mother, my sister, and I made up the force. Dad's job, until the shift ended, was in town.

Picking cotton is not easy work. It is, in fact, tortuously difficult. Sore knees and back, a fresh burn from the cooling but yet obstinate autumn sun, and swollen, scratched fingers were common, expected. This portion of the experience I did not particularly enjoy. But there was one part I did: the singing. We sang, old gospel songs mostly—"Farther Along", "On the Jericho Road", "Amazing Grace." Three parts—melody, alto, tenor. Probably would have been a strange and haunting sound had one happened upon the scene.

When fall glides quietly over the countryside and the harvest of cotton comes to mind, it is the singing I remember. Recollections of the discomforts are dim and far away.

There was another terrific attraction associated with fall cotton picking. That was to crawl onto a load of fresh cotton and tumble about in its softness, perhaps even ride home from the field while tucked into the white comfort. Is there anything like the smell and warmth of sunshine-fresh, hand picked cotton piled onto a wagon? I think not. If you have been so unfortunate as to miss this, you should yet take the time and expend the energy necessary to have that simple experience of ecstasy. Fall brings the euphoria of such moments to me.

Ripe muscadines were a part of autumn in childhood. Some of the most nectareous aromas and flavors known came from the cooking and subsequent eating of muscadine jelly. I can't resist the urge even now to gather a few ripe offerings from the muscadine vine, although more times than not these are never cooked and processed; they are simply fondled and admired. But just having them in the house for a brief time is comforting; is a certain signal of the advent of another resplendent autumn.

Squirrel hunting was an eagerly anticipated and much-heralded fall festivity; it remains as such. Cotton picking, muscadines, and squirrel hunting, if not concurrent, were close in their coming. And they came in autumn.

Squirrel hunting meant many things: the chill of early morning; the thrill of stalking a wily woods-dweller; the way my dad tilted his head to get the correct location of a barking bushytail; the crack of his worn 20-gauge; my mother's smile and nod of approval when we returned home with a future supper. Fall brings a revival and reliving of each; sadly these are only in memory. But what a vivid memory it is.

Autumn rekindles the feel and smell and heft of quilts—big, heavy, patchwork things that were pulled from overhead shelves, spread to sun, then thrown atop springy old beds with metal-tubing headboards. The frame house was less than tight against cold wind, and a quilt was the perfect addition. Autumns seemed cooler then than now.

You know what else quilts offer other than warmth? Security. So perhaps it is only imagined. There is still a measure of security in a quilt that is missing in a comforter or electric blanket or centrally-heated house. Fall brings with it that delightful security of quilts.

All these things—cotton, muscadines, squirrel hunting, quilts—are pleasant remembrances from another time. As age becomes an increasing impact more things are added, then catalogued away. All are immediate pleasantries sure to become treasured reflections if life goes on through next year and the next and the next. I, as you, have some more recent experiences to append to that long list from the past. Autumn now also means shimmering and rattling aspens that decorate a high-up and distant mountainside or creep down a draw to form an exaggerated exclamation point dotted with a sedgebrush "period." Their gold lasts only a few days, but those days are truly splendid.

It means, too, the blustery cold and first snow of the high country, the curious bounce of mule deer, that eerie screech of the bull elk. It means remote Canadian lakes bordered by tamarack bogs, clicking hooves of migrating caribou, outfitter tents beneath a cottonwood. These, coupled with those of yesterday, make each new autumn even more collectible than the one preceding it. Growing older, no doubt, plays an important role in the ability to recognize such matters, for one's sense of seeing the specialness of each day becomes more acute with age.

To fully appreciate autumn one should understand or at least exhibit some grasp of its contradictions. It is both the happiest and saddest of all times and all things.

Fall causes you to soar with pure exhiliration, then sink with melancholy. It is a time when weeping for the dead comes easily, a time to hold a child close and celebrate birth. Fall shouts loudly while it whispers softly.

I went for a walk today and realized a subtle but very real metamorphosis had swept the land and sky. Shadows lay at a peculiar angle in the woods, a tree-lined ditch with dry sand bottom was embellished by painted leaves, summer growth had lost the richness of its deep green. Another autumn had arrived.

It would be a time of distinction.

Kenner Patton

174

JANUARY OUT-OF-DOORS

Jim Ewing

This time of year brings on the bone-chilling weather, cold that cuts like a blade.

It's those freezing January sandpaper winds that can almost make your face bleed—rubbed raw. It's that January cold that can crush your toes into numbness, turn once-flexible fingers into senseless, twisted claws. It's that January cold that, if underestimated, can kill you—truly, finally, forever.

But it's also a welcome test of life to face such brutal cold—and survive. Without a testing of the body, the spirit can grow weak.

Our home fires are so welcome when coming in from a day spent out of doors in January's razor-like cold. It's a thankful kind of feeling.

Fires seem to burn better in the fireplace, like the flames eat the air better. Embers, though shorter-lived, burn hotter, it seems. They whistle a tuneless song of their very own, whispering a secret wisdom that invites long stares and reveries.

With January cold, simple acts are made more meaningful.

Eating from a steamy Thermos cup becomes almost a religious experience. Sipping hot coffee in the teeth of an icy gale is as welcome as a drowning man views breathing.

Spaces seem more wide open, like the air thins out. Sounds travel distances more easily, it seems. The trains on the midnight run through the cold and distant swamp sound more forlorn, their horns echo louder, lonelier, emptier, longer.

You imagine the owls and the feeding deer listening in fear and awe as those mighty night engines roar through the dark and issue their banshee winter wails, speeding along as if eager for warmth themselves.

Or, maybe we just notice them more—echoing our feelings in this killing cold time of year. They pass when we should be dreaming.

The outdoors is so awesome this time of year.

Those dawns. Some are like gray thieves of light, oozing a new day like a dull headache. They can dump surly rain and sleet on you, turn nasty and cold, or they can buffet you with benumbing winds.

Other dawns are glorious, colorful, deep, full and awesome, silent thunders of wonder, accompanied by a symphony of awakening life. The light can be so lucid—sharper, brighter—all the rising sun reveals appears surreal. Just looking is an experience. And watching the boiling steam from a roiling river melt hoarfrost in the trees is a sight not to be forgotten.

There's nothing like a January day to awaken latent ideas, reveal hidden thoughts, unveil new and important discoveries.

Sitting in a duck blind or on a deer stand when temperatures are freezing gives perspective to the common, everyday cares and concerns. Compared to clinging to life in death-dealing weather, those bills and bosses' whims don't mean much.

The warmth and comfort of simple conversation with a loved one at home is a luxury seldom appreciated more intently than while missing it, sitting on a cold stump with icicles forming on your nose.

But a wet lick on the face from a wet dog in a frozen duck swamp has its own beauty. It is in its way more precious than any amount of cash or fame.

A January day in the out-of-doors is a joy and a wonder to behold, as if its threat of quick, cold death makes living, warmth, and passion so much more valued and meaningful. It's great to be alive to enjoy another one!

176

THE WOLF AT OUR DOOR

David L. Watts

David Watts, Jackson, is a 16-year veteran with the Mississippi Department of Wildlife, Fisheries and Parks. He is editor of Mississippi Outdoors *magazine and treasurer for the Association for Conservation Information, Incorporated., an international organization for information and education professionals within the wildlife and natural resource fields.*

One airport lineman was overheard to remark, "This has got to be the most activity this little airport has seen in a long time." No doubt he was right. It is likely that Gulfpark Field had never witnessed quite the scene that took place there on this blustery January day. Some say that amid the excitement of the gathering press and media, somewhere crouched in the conversations of visiting scientists and biologists, there was a little bit of conservation history in the making.

What happened is really very simple. On this overcast, winter afternoon, state and federal agencies were bringing in a pair of red wolves to live and hopefully breed on nearby Horn Island. And in a broader context, what was going on signaled far-reaching implications for a wildlife species now known to be extinct in its former range. But, perhaps, in a more general sense, a portion of mankind reached beyond itself in a good faith effort to bring itself into harmony with the greater forces of nature.

It was shortly after 4:00 p.m. when a twin-engine airplane of the National Park Service landed at Ocean Springs. Among those aboard were

Roland Smith, Assistant Director of the Point Defiance Zoo and Aquarium in Tacoma, Washington, and biologist Warren Parker of the U.S. Fish and Wildlife Service in North Carolina. Smith has been considered one of the foremost authorities in America on the red wolf. Parker, a nearly 30-year veteran with the Service, was the team leader for the national recovery effort to bring this wolf back from near oblivion. Also aboard in two separate cages were a male and female red wolf, flown here from their former home at the Alligator River National Wildlife Refuge in North Carolina.

Authorities had pre-arranged to have the aircraft taxi into one of the airport's two hangars and have the doors closed, all in an effort to prevent escape in the unlikely event that the muzzled wolves somehow managed to struggle free. On hand witnessing all this were representatives of the local press and media, officials from state and federal agencies, and others.

Shortly after deplaning, Roland Smith explained briefly to the press what was about to happen as he and Parker transferred the wolves from the aircraft to separate canine kennels. Within a matter of minutes and in a no-nonsense manner, the men placed each wolf in a kennel, ready for the nearly one-hour boat ride to Horn Island, one of the few genuine stretches of wilderness left in the Magnolia state.

On a clear day you can stand on the shore at Bellefontaine Beach near Ocean Springs and look south-southeast, and you will spot one of the crown jewels of wilderness retreat in Mississippi. A piece of the South Seas at our back door. A place where the offshore sounds of silence are brought to echo among the sand spits by the lap of sea on shore and the rustle of wind-swept pines atop towering dunes. Welcome to Horn Island.

Here is a barrier island existence that is, for all practical purposes, left to the wiles of nature. A fit existence only for man's occasional visit, and a home for the likes of cottonmouth moccasin and moorhen, wild boar and boat-tailed grackle, Eastern meadowlarks and—wolves? Wolves. At least for now and possibly for the future. A fit setting for a wolf propagation program, and it is here that the two red wolves were brought after a one-hour boat ride from Ocean Springs.

By the time officials accompanying the animals arrived on the island, it was night. The wolves were quickly carried to an undisclosed location where the National Park Service had constructed a 50-foot-square holding pen. Both Smith and Parker closely examined the structure and said that it should hold the animals until they were ready to be released the next day. However, both agreed that since it was night and the wolves were in a strange location, it would be safer to release them from the kennels in the morning.

The next day officials met on Horn Island for a workshop conducted by Roland Smith in handling and caring for the wolves. In his matter-of-fact way, Smith emphasized that the wolves were to be dealt with in an authoritative manner, and that once inside the holding pen, it was all serious business.

"You must remember that there is only one part of a wolf that can really hurt you, and that's its mouth," Smith emphasized.

"These animals can bite you so fast that it's very important to keep your mind on what you are doing, and to coordinate your actions with the others helping you."

Next, under Smith and Parker's watchful eye, those that would be handling the wolves for the next several months practiced removing each animal from its kennel and returning it. Finally, after the basic capture techniques had been reviewed, the kennel doors were opened, and the wolves loped out into their new holding-pen home.

Certainly for the next few months, this enclosure on Mississippi's most beautiful wilderness island would be home to two creatures representing a species struggling to survive. This pair of wolves, two of only about 89 remaining individuals of their kind, hopefully would mate and produce a litter of wild-reared pups. If this cooperative venture succeeds, officials will transfer the young back to their parent's original home on Alligator River National Wildlife Refuge.

State Department of Wildlife Conservation biologist Will McDearman of Jackson was confident that the wolves would survive nicely on Horn Island. "This innovative program provided important and new knowledge that advanced other conservation programs intended to insure the survival of this species."

McDearman was probably more prophetic in his thinking than he chose to imagine. Because what most Americans may have failed to comprehend is that the red wolf was near extinction. This animal, once one of the principal carnivores in Mississippi and the Southeast, was now the area's most endangered mammal. With so few red wolves believed to exist, these remaining canids were literally struggling to survive. And make no mistake about it—extinction is forever.

But why had this wolf—one of the premiere examples of wilderness, of the survival of the fittest—why has it fared so poorly over time? And how did it arrive at its precarious lot in life? Did its past reveal it to be so unadaptable and yielding to man and his times? In short, was anyone to blame for all this, or was nature merely taking its course?

The red wolf (*Canis rufus*) once was distributed rather widely over portions of North America in the early to middle Pleistocene (the Ice Age). Some authorities say that gradually other animals and a changing environment may have caused the red wolf to retreat into the marshes, swamps, and extensive forests of the Southeast and portions of the Atlantic Coast. But it wasn't until the arrival of white settlers in this country that the red wolf faced its real test of survival.

As settlers migrated to America, they brought with them many of the superstitious beliefs and mysterious legends that had surrounded the wolf in Europe for years. From certainly the Dark Ages and maybe before, there persisted twisted rumors of wolves carrying off babies and in general

180

causing havoc among rural peasants. No doubt medieval clerics enhanced and perpetuated the notion that the wolf embodied the very essence of the devil's evil spirit. As history has so demonstrated, the wolf was getting a bad rap from the beginning.

Then as tidewater pioneers gradually overcame the initial hurdle of the Appalachian Mountains, they set their sights on settling and taming western lands. There they found the red wolf and other large predators in areas from Florida west to Texas and northward to the Ohio River Valley. And it was here that the wolf began its slow exit toward extinction from its historic native range.

"The early extermination of wolves on the Atlantic seaboard was the result of an ancient attitude," noted wolf authority Ronald M. Nowak said.

"Striking out of the river swamps, their howls piercing the night, these animals probably seemed like devils incarnate to the early settler with his European background."

Nowak and others have suggested that man had a basic fear of the wolf, even though there are no thoroughly documented cases of wolves killing people. Farmers and settlers entering new territories were concerned about depredation from wolves on their domestic livestock, although other elements of nature probably took a greater toll of animal life. Early outdoorsmen believed wolves to be unnecessary predators on big game animals. Man and his advancing civilization was becoming a force that would ultimately deal with the wolf on man's terms. Said Nowak, "In his relationship with the wolf, man seems to have believed that he was dealing not with an ordinary natural problem, but with an enemy that had to be destroyed."

Since man's first movement into the Southeast, his removal and clearing of vast tracts of bottomland hardwoods for his cities, roads, and other conveniences have been deciding factors in the fate of red wolves and other large carnivores like the bear and the panther. Through his continued efforts at trapping, poisoning, and dynamiting, man was unrelenting in forcing the red wolf into smaller and smaller remote areas for survival.

It has been said by some that wolves maintained an existence in the mountains of Virginia and North Carolina until early in the twentieth century. Florida and Georgia were reporting a few red wolves in certain remote areas in 1920. By 1940 the range of the red wolf had been vastly reduced in numbers since the species was suspected to be hybridizing with the coyote. In Mississippi the last red wolf was collected by the federal government in Claiborne County in 1946.

It probably was not until the environmental awareness of the 1960s that scientists began to realize that everything was not right with the red wolf. Biologists were discovering that the true red wolf was being replaced by a hybrid cross between it and the coyote. Finally, the precarious nature of the wolf warranted authorities placing the animal on the federal endangered species list in January 1965. And by the early 1970s a recovery program had been set up by the U.S. Fish and Wildlife Service, of which captive breeding became a part.

After the plight of the red wolf became fully known, it was decided early on that a captive breeding project would be one way to take a stock of genetically pure red wolves, breed them in captivity to increase their numbers, and hopefully build up sufficient numbers to one day re-establish the species in at least a portion of its natural range. So from the outset, the Fish and Wildlife Service set as its goal something that had never been done before in America. We're talking the successful reintroduction of a predator into the wild.

In November 1973 a captive breeding project was arranged with the Point Defiance Zoo and Aquarium in Tacoma under the supervision of Assistant Director Roland Smith. Red wolves were rounded up from known areas of existence and shipped to the Tacoma facility, with the last one arriving in March 1979. Then in the fall of 1980, scientists considered the red wolf to be extinct in the wild.

According to one source on the red wolf, the first recorded litters of red wolves were produced in captivity in the spring of 1977. The captive breeding project, of which Horn Island had been a part, made a significant contribution to conservation history when, in September 1987, two red wolves which had been born and reared in captivity were released on the Alligator River National Wildlife Refuge. A species known to be extinct in the wild had been returned to a portion of its historic range. And so with success under its belt, the Service expanded the scope of its breeding project to take in Horn Island. They hoped that success on Horn, much like that experienced with red wolves on Bulls Island in South Carolina in the late 1970s, would provide a source of wild pups for further re-introductions and captive breedings, as well as yield valuable data on the biology of red wolves and associated predator-prey relationships.

Biologists like Will McDearman got excited about this project, confident that the project and the wolves would do well on Horn Island. "Horn is located some seven miles off the Mississippi coastline, and being a wilderness barrier island, the wolves should readily find what they need to exist there," McDearman said.

Horn Island certainly seemed a good choice for a red wolf propagation experiment. Previous biological studies involving wolves on islands, such as those with gray wolves, showed promising results. And in 1978 the Fish and Wildlife Service demonstrated success with red wolves on Bulls Island in South Carolina. If the wolves on Horn Island didn't survive, it would not be because the island could not meet their living requirements.

Located less than ten miles off the Mississippi coastline, Horn is a wilderness island maintained by the National Park Service. Upwards of three-fourths of a mile wide and some 13 miles long, the 3,700-acre island is an environmental mixture of sand dunes and swamps, rice rats and rabbits. And more. A number of freshwater ponds and sloughs occur throughout the island's central section. Predators like the wolf would find adequate food available in the island's population of cottontail rabbits, nutria, raccoons, and rodents. Besides the wolves, no other mammal predators existed on Horn Island.

With a red wolf study underway, there were questions as to continued public access to Horn Island. Park Service plans called for the island to remain open to public use during the period. But they asked that people visiting the island respect the closed area around the wolf holding pen and not trespass. Visitors in this area could unnecessarily disturb the animals.

Over the hundreds of years in which wolves and men have faced each other, there has developed a precarious love-hate relationship. Once thought to be the earthly embodiment of Satan risen from the bowels of hell, the wolf fell on hard times from almost the beginning. The legacy of the wolf as one of America's powerful predators has come counter to man's innuendo and harassment, but not before succumbing with a terrible toll. Civilization's cunning at trapping, killing, and outright no-holds-barred attempts to rid itself of a magnificent reminder of wilderness has come close to success.

But in our efforts at what some would say was controlling the wolf, we have discovered what others might suggest is a higher responsibility. And that is that our stewardship of planet Earth is an accountability of what the natural world offers us. We have come counter to all this by re-introducing the red wolf into the wild. We have arrived at the realization that the culmination of our culture is perhaps not measured so much in what we have defeated or destroyed, but rather in what we have accommodated in our quest to survive and succeed. That is the past and the future of the red wolf.

CLEANLINESS IS NEXT TO WHAT?!!!!

Robert Hitt Neill

T he Great Outdoors is not a particularly clean place, as most of us who
venture outside know. There's sand, weeds, dirt which turns to mud
or dust with the whims of the weather, bugs, spiders and their webs,
and other impediments to Clean Living to be encountered just on a short
hike into the woods. On camping expeditions, or even a simple church
outing for the evening, the campfire smoke always stings one's eyes and
pungently scents hair, clothes, and equipment. Ashes on a hot dog, sand
on the marshmallows, and bugs in the stew are Outdoor Givens. A fishing
trip of only a couple of hours requires one's hand to become tainted with
the intimate inside juices of worms, crickets, roaches, and even the fish
themselves. Cleaning game after a successful hunt involves both sweat and
blood.

As the saying goes, "It's a dirty job, but someone's got to do it!"

Hunters, fishermen, campers, hikers, and canoers often will leave
civilization and force themselves to endure these conditions for days, or
even weeks, at a time. Now, while there are some camps which are
Cadillacs, so to speak, many others are just Edsels and Studebakers, where
conditions are relatively primitive. There ain't no room service, much less
inside plumbing.

These conditions are understood and accepted by most outdoorsmen;
indeed, sometimes they are unneccessarily harkened back to. For instance,
I was never allowed to forget the time we first installed running water and
a hot water heater in our rustic cabin. After five days of deer hunting, I
showered, shaved, and splashed on smellgood before we broke camp and

headed for home. Took three months to allay her suspicions, and I've never shaved at camp again!

This type misunderstanding is a wonderful justification for including the ladies in the outdoor activities, if possible. If your wife will accompany you on hunting trips and suchlike, I encourage you to make arrangements for her participation. However, I must warn those husbands who enjoy the comfort of a cabin out in the boondocks: wives approach these accommodations with a different standard of cleanliness than their husbands. A lady can walk into a hunting cabin considered virtually spotless by any of the male occupants who stoop to consider such things, and exclaim, "My lands! When was the last time this place was cleaned up?!!"

Do not take offense; this is simply a Rule of Nature. Women are just different from men, and praise the Lord for it!

My suggestion in these cases is to plan on arriving at camp by at least the middle of the afternoon before Opening Day, deposit your lady at the cabin for the inevitable observation, and explain that you must depart for the woods to scout the hunting area before nightfall. She will be perfectly content in your absence; just be sure that you are quite vocal in your admiration of the spotless abode upon your return to start supper.

Showering, or bathing, is an activity that really is called for at times during camping trips. For instance, a fellow gets up in the cold dawn, dons long-johns, insulateds, flannels, woolens, and other clothes designed to keep him from freezing, and heads for the woods. By noon, a warm front has come through, the temperature is up to sixty, and our hero has a 150-pound ten-point buck to drag out to the road.

We're talking major sweat here, and for an extended period of time. Then the buck must be loaded into the jeep and, since the weather has turned warm, must be skinned out back at camp, quartered, and the meat packed into ice chests for preservation. By this time, the afternoon hunt is nearly over, and someone has to catch up the hounds, feed the horses, cut some firewood, and start supper. After three days of this type activity, you could swear that a family of skunks has set up housekeeping in the bottom end of your sleeping bag.

But the sleeping bag itself is not the problem; it is merely a symptom. Bedding can be aired during the day and made tolerable. It is crawling into that bag with yourself that becomes intolerable.

A couple of us reached that point one November at deer camp and vowed that we were going to bathe in the Mississippi River, in spite of the fact that the water temperature was a chilly fifty degrees. Armed with soap, towels, and clean clothes, we cranked the jeep and headed for the riverbank sandbar. Bear in mind that this was miles from any co-educational civilization. Just a couple of us boys around, and an occasional towboat in the river channel, which was maybe 250 yards away. At that distance, no one could even determine gender, much less detail.

We shed our clothes and long-johns at the jeep and, with soap and towels, walked to the river's edge. The plan was to lather up good in the ankle-deep water by the sandbar, then run out to greater depth, submerge, rinse, and run back to our towels, thus minimizing exposure to the cold river water. As we began working up a lather, a towboat rounded the bend upstream, unnoticed by us, though it made no difference to The Plan, because of distance. Finally, sudsy from head to toe, we pitched our soap toward the jeep and turned to the water. "Last one in is a rotten egg!" I bellowed. We charged into the river, anticipating the cold but cleansing shock.

And kept charging. Unbeknownst to us, the dog-gone sandbar was only ankle-deep for nearly 200 yards.

"Yeeeeeee-haaaaaaa!!" Our Rebel Yells attracted the attention of the towboat crew as we sprinted through the shallows, suds flying. The forward lookout waved toward the bridge, pointing.

"Yeeeeeee-Haaaaaaa!" we yelled, knowing the next step would surely be deeper. The Captain moved to the starboard wing and raised his binoculars.

"Yeeeee-haaaaa!" still ankle-deep we charged. The deck crew lined the starboard rail as the towboat's whistle blew a salute.

"Yeeee-haaaa!" I could feel the suds drying as we raced onward. The ship's cook stepped from the galley, wiping her hands on her apron.

"Yeee-haaa!" was sounding hoarse and forced as we ran. The Captain's wife joined him on the wing of the bridge and reached for the binoculars.

"Yee-haa!" was becoming a scream of desperation as goose bumps pushed soapsuds from our bodies, while what seemed to be the soprano section of the Mormon Tabernacle Choir began emerging from the crew's quarters.

"Ye-ha!" What next?

Mercifully, less than fifty yards from the towboat, our feet finally hit deeper water as the crowds cheered. We raised our heads from rinsing just in time to hear the first mate bellow, "Whatever it was, it ain't chasin' you no more!"

We sprinted back. Cleansed.

Yet once the hunters' bodies are fully cleansed from the rigors of the trip, there remains a job that usually falls to the lady of the house. It is not really fair that all those filthy garments must be rendered acceptable for polite society again by one who does not regularly enjoy the trips, but sometimes a wife and mother learns the hard way not to trust her menfolks with complicated household appliances.

It was actually a rather natural thing to do, I tried to explain to calm her down. Matter of fact, most teenage boys would have been had up for being helpful beyond the call of duty, I pointed out. Surely she appreciated the situation wherein a couple of dove hunters who had been caught in the rain thought better than to just leave their sopping hunting shirts in the middle of the floor? How many youngsters would be considerate enough to stick the wet camo shirts into the dryer, saving their mamas all that time and trouble?

To be honest, it had not been the boy who had done the deed. However, I learned a long time ago that when the lady of the house reaches a certain degree of temper, it is usually best to blame things on someone who is out of reach. In the present case, the boy was now over a hundred miles away at college. Discretion is sometimes the better part of valor, and I could always 'fess up after she cooled down.

Doves are different from most game birds in that they are about two hundred percent feathers. These feathers are just barely attached to the bird's body—a hunter can literally blow on his limit of doves to pick them, except for wing and tail feathers. Many retrievers only work on doves under protest, for the feathers come off in the dog's mouth so easily. Yank used to deliver my doves reproachfully, afterwards spitting out wads of distasteful grey fluff. The fact that this loose attachment is really an advantage in dove cleaning was completely lost on my Labrador.

It was also lost on Betsy when she opened the dryer. One dove had been overlooked in one pocket of one shirt by one hunter.

This dove was now completely picked, ready for easy cleaning and cooking. However, my instincts told me that it would probably not be in my best interests to point this out to my wife, at least not right now. Yet it has since occurred to me that there may well be a new commercial application here.

If one does not hunt doves (or is not married to a dove hunter), one could not imagine the amount of feathers in that dryer. They burst out when the door was opened; they permeated (and penetrated!) all of the clothes; they stuck out from all those little holes in the dryer where I guess the hot air comes in; they packed the filter in layers. I was later to learn that skivvy shorts washed with dove feathers cause embarrassing itches in places that cannot be scratched in dignified company.

Since quality outdoor books usually include some tips on game cookery for their readers, perhaps I could offer the Neill Family Recipe for Dried Dove:

One (1) Dove; uncleaned, but freshly deceased

One (1) electric clothes dryer

One (1) small load of men's underwear (freshly cleaned) *Note: Women's underwear might work just as well as far as the dove is concerned, but I suspect would greatly multiply the number and coverage of embarrassing itches, perhaps leading to the liberation and burning of these garments.*

CAUTION: Do not use long-johns!!

Directions: place dove and underwear in dryer under low heat for one (1) hour or until the filter stops up. Remove dove, dress (not in underwear), and roast on grill for twenty (20) minutes wrapped in a strip of bacon.

Donate underwear to Salvation Army (notify your accountant for proper tax deductions).

Clean filter.

By the way, this recipe also makes for an interesting side dish: Steamed Wife!!

LISTENING FOR A SHOT

Mabry Anderson

L ately I spend much of my time on deer stands listening for shots, rather than concentrating on bagging a buck of my own. This probably happens to most of us who rear sons and daughters who follow in our footsteps. As we grow older, our concern for the success of others grows stronger.

Sitting in the winter woods, watching and listening to the sounds of the forest becomes the real purpose of the hunt, and a day that I like to remember was very much this way.

For the Deep South, this day was particularly cold, the December woods were stark and dead, and the hard white frost and glaring ice on standing water were reminiscent of woods far to the north rather than the lower delta of the Mississippi River. Regardless of season, these woods are always beautiful: the towering wild pecan, stark white cottonwood, and colorful maple blending perfectly with low-growing box elder, ironwood, hackberry, and scattered persimmon. Where game is concerned, this is a land of plenty, a small wilderness encompassed by the levee on the east and the channel of the river to the west. Scattered cultivated fields punctuate the forest, planted usually to soybeans and winter wheat, and forest game, particularly deer and turkey, is found in great abundance.

Logging activities, while disturbing from an aesthetic view, have probably done much toward bringing about a great increase in game. The low-growing food plants produced by selective cutting have exploded the whitetail population to a point where our main problem is harvesting enough animals to prevent overpopulation. This restricted area lies on both sides of the river and is made up of portions of Mississippi, Arkansas, and Louisiana, and although most of it is privately owned and controlled by hunting clubs, it still offers superb hunting to thousands of sportsmen.

On this particular morning, both of my now-grown children were with me: my son, Mabry, a long-legged 6-foot-3 who had been a woodsman almost since infancy, and my blonde daughter, Vicki, equally at home in the woods and capable of taking care of herself under almost all circumstances. I had dropped them off at their respective stands and driven the four-wheel drive deeper into the winter woods to a favorite spot that overlooked several well-worn deer crossings. A huge downed pecan had fallen in exactly the right spot and it was my habit to climb its elevated trunk some 30 feet or more and sit comfortably against one of its giant lower limbs that offered an excellent back rest. Viewing was perfect; you could see clearly for several hundred yards in all directions, over and beyond the low vegetation that surrounded the tree. When I walked the last few steps to the stand, several flashing white-tails bounced away through the brush, but I paid them little mind, knowing that many deer would soon be moving, either from dog action or from other hunters.

The traditional hounding of deer, long associated with Southern hunting, has fallen off greatly during the past few years. Time was when good dogs were a necessity and back then, with a scarcity of deer, a good hound was often hard put to strike a hot trail even once a day. Times change, and nowadays any old dog will quickly blunder into a herd of deer, scattering them in many directions, and a really good race usually never develops. Occasionally a big buck will pull out of the herd and a wise hound or two will single him out and initiate a decent race—but not often. What usually happens is that the hounds will move a drove of deer through the woods and very shortly run into another herd so that they are soon widely scattered all over the big, flat country with the pack completely disintegrated. Actually this makes very little difference since white-tails often follow well-known trails and if a hunter merely sits and waits, he will usually score.

Thoughts kept crowding in as I sat and waited, and I recalled the day that my son bagged his first buck from a stand not a quarter-mile from where I was sitting.

His ninth birthday was only two days past that morning, and perhaps he was a bit young for hunting. He was clutching his little 20-gauge tightly as we sat together on a fallen log when suddenly, I made out the sound of hounds moving our way.

"You hear those dogs, son?" I murmured. "They're coming our way, so sit tight and watch toward the south."

Suddenly I saw the deer, a big spike, running well ahead of the hounds and coming straight to us. At a dead run, that buck was on us almost immediately, and, without a word from me, Mabry leveled that 20-gauge and let fly with a load of No. 4 buck. The deer literally died in midstride; he never knew what hit him.

By now the sun was well up and the frost was slowly vanishing. From the north I could hear the faint sound of hounds and suddenly, without actually realizing it, I was looking at several deer skulking through the brush directly toward me. Several does with yearlings and one small four-point buck walked right by, and I let them pass.

Turkeys began calling nearby and in a moment I saw them, a great flock of perhaps forty birds, evidently several groups of the year with their respective mothers. They moved along slowly, scratching for pecans that are a winter staple. Turkeys can move like ghosts. They are capable of walking through dry sycamore leaves without making a sound and I sat there with my heart pounding as they fed to within 20 steps of my stand. No old longbeards were present, the entire drove being comprised of young and a few old hens guiding them along with maternal clucks.

Several does drifted by, along with one spike buck, but still nothing of real interest. At times like this, I begin to wonder just what I am doing out here myself. Surely there must be things to do, but somehow they don't seem to matter just now. The woods hold a special sort of appeal and I am persuaded that a great deal of my time must be spent there, in spite of the fact that some consider this to be time wasted. I can't believe it, especially when I recall red-letter days like the one when my daughter brought down her first really good buck and did it all alone.

Like most fathers, I usually insisted that we sit together with me calling the shots, but on this particular morning, she had other ideas.

"Dad, this time I'm going my way and you and Mabry go yours. Not that I don't like your company, but I just want to hunt alone this morning."

With misgivings, we followed her orders. Something about a girl child brings out the protective instinct in both fathers and brothers, and I remember how small she looked when we left her sitting there in the cold dawn, armed with her .243, a king-sized cola, and a couple of cupcakes.

"Do you reckon she'll be all right?" murmured my son and without really believing it, I nodded my assent, as we plodded along to our own stands a quarter of a mile further on.

At times like this, you do nothing except listen for a shot. Dogs were well scattered that morning and deer were moving freely, but I was not at all concerned with bagging one. Time dragged, and after allowing a six-pointer to walk by, I considered walking to her stand for a visit. Instead, I walked to Mabry's stand where we sat together, drinking coffee and listening.

A shot rang out and we knew perfectly well that it was her. The peculiar flat crack of the .243 is unmistakable, and we jumped to our feet.

"Reckon she's shot herself?" muttered Mabry, not entirely facetiously, and, with uneasy grins, we headed for her stand. A half-minute later another shot rang out, this one muffled, and we knew what had happened.

She must have knocked down a deer and then run up and finished him off with a shot through the neck...at least we hoped so.

Finally we broke into the opening where we'd left her and there she was, one foot on the neck of a really fine eight-pointer, and seeming to have grown in stature since we left her at dawn!

"He was coming right down that trail," she bubbled, "and I just sort of felt him being there before I saw him! When I looked around, there he was, behind that brush with just his head and neck showing. I eased up the rifle but couldn't find him in the scope but then he took a step or two and when he did, I caught his neck in the scope and let fly."

The extra shot through the neck was completely unnecessary, the first one having broken the spine. He never knew that she was around at all.

By now the morning was almost gone. As I debated about climbing down and visiting the kids, a flicker of movement to my right caught my attention and, in the heavy brush, I could see a big doe standing stock-still and looking back down the trail behind her. Watching carefully, I then saw another deer, head down with only his flank exposed, almost completely obscured by a small thicket of elderberry bushes, evidently feeding or sniffing along at ground level. For at least a minute, both deer just stood there, and then, as the doe took a step toward me, the other one moved forward a few yards and raised his head. He was not the biggest buck on earth, but a real trophy and, as he stood there perfectly still, I slowly raised the rifle and centered the crosshairs on his neck just below the ear line.

A big buck is a magnificent creature with his antlers glinting in the winter sunlight. Finally, almost reluctantly, I squeezed the trigger, and at the crack of the rifle he simply disappeared from view. The 100-grain .243 Spitzer driving along at more than 3,000 feet per second seldom allows your target another step if your aim is right. Very deliberately I crawled down from my stand and trudged through the crackling leaves to where he had fallen.

He lay there just as I knew he would be, as fine an eight-pointer as any man could ask for. Evidently this was to be my day. Although I had listened carefully for shots from my kids, none had materialized, and since the morning was about gone, I suspected that the hunt was over.

As always, I examined my buck with mixed emotions. I knew for a moment with great certainty that were I to become omnipotent for a day, with a wave of my hand I would bring this buck back to life and watch as he bounced away through the trees. But being only a man, I lacked that power, so with a sigh, I slowly began the task of field dressing him.

I deliberately lingered over the job because I knew that, in a very short while, I'd have plenty of help from two different sources. Already those kids were on their way—my son sneaking along Indian-fashion, his black cowboy hat bobbing in the brush, and my daughter, blonde hair streaming and red coat flapping, literally trotting through the woods on the way to my stand.

It always works out this way. Dads are not the only people who sit on stands listening for shots. Sons and daughters do it too, and as I laid out my buck, I heard them coming, and somehow it made all of that "wasted" time well worthwhile.

196

Shade Steele

WHEN THE TIME WAS MINE

Paul Meek

Paul Meek, Morton, is the owner of "Paul Meek Hunting Products" and manufactures calls, scents, and other outdoor products. He writes poetry and outdoor stories as a hobby.

May it always be as it was when the time was mine.
May my children hear the sounds of the hounds in pursuit, in the still, frosty, morning time.
Let them hear the bark of the squirrel as the autumn leaves begin to fall.
And know in their hearts, God, that you created it all.
Let them hear the wind as it sings thru the pines, and smell the richness of your forest,
As I did in my time.
May my children's children as they grow and the time is theirs,
Breathe the freshness of your forest's air.
Let them hear the ring of the gobbler in the spring,
Smell the powder and hear the shotgun as it sings.
Let them thrill to the hunt, but make them understand.
This is a gift given, but one no man can demand.
Let them grow to be my eyes and ears when I am old and bent—my time all spent.
So we may share all these things that were heaven sent.
And it comes to be when the time is no longer mine.
Would you Lord, protect them and keep them as you did me,
When the time was mine.

Shade Steele